The Korean War

The
Korean
War

Edited with an Introduction by

Lloyd C. Gardner

A NEW YORK TIMES BOOK

Quadrangle Books

A NEW YORK TIMES COMPANY

DS
919
.G37
1972

Library of Congress Catalog Card Number: 72–130383
International Standard Book Number:
  Cloth 0–8129–0249–1
  Paper 0–8129–6193–5

The publishers are grateful to the contributors
herein for permission to reprint their articles.

B379865

Contents

2. A Time of Testing

3. Reflections on Past and Future

The Korean War

Introduction

Thus far we have temporized and improvised. Our time for that ran out when North Korean tanks crossed the border. We can lose half a world at this point if we lose heart.

New York Times, *editorial,*
June 26, 1950

AMERICANS WENT into the Korean War having been told that the fate of Asia and perhaps of the world hung in the balance. Although the nation's military planners had concluded that Korea itself was of little strategic importance to the United States, and that nothing there warranted risking a land war on a peninsula next to the Chinese and Russian mainlands, a divided Korea had nonetheless become an ideological battleground in the Cold War. At the time, American policy-makers assumed that the Soviets had "unleashed" the war, but their specific aims in doing so have never been fully explained. The Truman administration mooted the question, claiming that American intervention was justified to prevent further encroachment on the "Free World." It made little difference what motivated the North Koreans anyway, since the ultimate aim of all communists was supposed to be world conquest.

The articles reprinted here faithfully reflect this policy-making consensus and the prevailing sense of urgency surrounding the decision to take a stand in Korea.

Waging a Cold War was hard on the nerves. Korea at last offered some real battle lines. In less time than it took President Harry S. Truman to fly back to Washington from his home in Missouri, the administration put aside its doubts and readied itself for the tasks ahead. Truman himself had made up his mind what to do almost immediately upon hearing of the North Korean attack. As he boarded the *Independence* for the return flight, an aide confided to a nearby reporter, "The boss is going to hit those fellows hard." Those fellows were the North Koreans, about 75,000 of them, who, with the support of Russian-built tanks, were rapidly moving down on Seoul, the capital of South Korea.

Truman was certainly aware that in reacting strongly he would also be striking a blow against Republican critics who had been badgering his administration about its Asian policies. Their most serious charge was that Chiang Kai-shek had been sold out by the Democrats in a series of decisions going back to the Yalta Conference of the Big Three in 1945. Republican criticisms undoubtedly played some part in Truman's decision to overrule the Joint Chiefs of Staff, who had repeatedly warned against becoming involved in Korea; it is difficult to assess this domestic political influence, or to isolate it from the general concern that if the United States did not accept the challenge in Korea, the Soviets' next move would come in Europe or the Middle East.

Some policy-makers felt that Japan was the real communist objective. The conquest of Korea, coming so soon after the "loss" of China, was to be part of an international psychological campaign to push Japan into neutralism, and then into communism, almost without firing a shot. With such matters to consider, policy-makers did not pay much attention to the political situation in Korea itself as a cause of the war. Neither the *New York Times* editorial of June 26, 1950, nor Truman's speech to the nation the following day noted this factor as having any bearing on the crisis. Truman had been briefed on the internal tensions in Korea on several occasions, but he apparently discounted their importance except as local Cold War symptoms. Without the Cold War there would have been no Korean War; yet without the Korean War, American Far Eastern policies in succeeding years would have been difficult to justify.

The invasion began at dawn on June 25, 1950, Korean time, or shortly after 8 P.M., June 24, in Washington. The story came over the wires of the United Press. Official confirmation from the American Embassy in Seoul did not reach the State Department for another hour and a half, consequently the American public learned of the attack at about the same time, or before 11:20 P.M., when Secretary of State Dean Acheson put through a call to the President. "Mr. President," began Acheson, "I have very serious news. The North Koreans have invaded South Korea."

Acheson advised against the President's immediate return to Washington since further details would not be available for several hours. He also suggested calling for an emergency session of the United Nations Security Council. Later congressional hearings would reveal that the State Department had been working on a new proposal to get around the Soviet veto power in the Security Council for some time before the Korean crisis. When Truman agreed to ask for a Security Council meeting, State Department drafters went to work on a number of related resolutions. No one in the building with Acheson that evening believed that the North Koreans would obey a "cease and desist" order from the world organization, but it was the proper way to set things in motion. Meanwhile, other drafters began work on the text of a resolution requesting UN members to furnish "such assistance . . . as may be necessary" to the victim, the American-sponsored Republic of Korea.

Everything went smoothly—even too smoothly. The resolution request for UN aid passed on Tuesday, June 27, with Yugoslavia casting a lone negative vote. Egypt and India abstained. None of these three possessed the veto power. Russia did, but, curiously enough, its delegate, Jacob Malik, was currently boycotting all

Security Council meetings to protest the continued presence of the Chinese Nationalist delegate. His absence permitted quick action by the UN, but it deprived the United States of an expected opportunity to take the issue to the General Assembly, where it hoped to limit the Soviet veto power.*

In the first weeks after the invasion, Truman told the American people that "The attack upon Korea makes it plain beyond all doubt that Communism has passed beyond the use of subversion to conquer independent nations, and will now use armed invasion and war." Yet he avoided blaming the Soviet Union directly. Why the distinction? Was it simply meant as a diplomatic signal to the Russians, as later explanations would have it, so that Moscow might have one final chance to halt the adventure before it was too late? The explanation seems logical enough, but it is self-serving and must be examined carefully. The State Department's initial soundings of Moscow's intentions brought responses which satisfied the experts that Korea was in fact *not* the prelude to a general Soviet offensive. But no one in the United States government corrected or amended the President's assertion that the Russians had passed beyond subversion to armed invasion and war. Indeed, the Assistant Secretary of State for Public Affairs, Edward W. Barrett, epitomized the administration's continuing approach to "homefront" diplomacy with the statement that the relationship between the Soviet Union and the North Koreans was like that between "Walt Disney and Donald Duck."

* The United States had planned to introduce in the General Assembly, and see passed, a "Uniting for Peace" resolution, which would have taken the matter out of the Security Council's hands. A few months later the American delegate in the General Assembly formally introduced the resolution anyway, citing the Korean situation as an example of the need to be sure that in future crises there was some way for the organization to act without big-power unanimity. Passed by a vote of 52 to 5, the "Uniting for Peace" resolution was the first concrete political gain for the United States resulting from the Korean War. And it was a big one, for, in effect, the proposal changed the structure and nature of the United Nations by affirming new powers for the General Assembly. Stymied by Soviet vetos in the Security Council over the preceding four years, the United States had seemingly made the UN into an effective "collective security" organization.

Barrett was told by higher officials to pipe down, but not because they wished to allow the Soviets a chance to save face by calling off the attack. Barrett was ordered to avoid comments on the relationship between Moscow and Pyongyang because the State Department was anxious to assure the Russians that America's objectives were limited to repelling the invaders. From the beginning, the Korean War was to have all the complications of a John LeCarré plot, with the leading characters on the American political scene every bit as complex as those in LeCarré's Cold War novels. This brings up, again, the question of the President's phrasing of his June 27 message to the American people: Was it worded so that the nation would respond *as if* Korea were a signal to communists everywhere? Three years before, in the 1947 Greek-Turkish crisis, Truman had been advised by Republican Senator Arthur H. Vandenberg that he would have to "scare hell" out of the country if he expected Congress to appropriate the money to save those areas from communism. Perhaps having once accepted such advice, Truman saw no alternative to using it in a new Cold War crisis. Or perhaps he felt justified in using such language regardless of expert opinion on Soviet motives, because any hint of appeasement would only lead to a world crisis later. Whatever the reasons, and there was most certainly a mixture of several, Truman applied Vandenberg's maxim to the fullest at the outset of the Korean situation. He deliberately created a sense of impending disaster, even referring to Korea as the "Greece of the Far East."

At the first post-invasion congressional briefing, hours before he spoke to the nation, the President pulled out all the stops: "This act was very obviously inspired by the Soviet Union. If we let Korea down, the Soviet will keep on going and swallow up one piece of Asia after another." If Asia went, the Near East would soon begin to crumble. There was "no telling" what would happen in Europe. Now was the time, perhaps the last chance, to draw the line: not alone in Korea, but in Indochina, the Philippines, and Formosa. There was no ambiguity in this "off the record" discussion with legislative leaders. However one interprets the President's

June 27 message to the nation, it is clear that he was anxious for a big public response, big enough to help resolve other problems besides Korea.

Before the North Korean attack, each of the three Asian countries the President had mentioned posed a special problem. Formosa was the newest trouble spot. It had been assumed—too easily, it turned out—that the island would simply revert to Chinese rule at the end of World War II. American military authorities were carrying out this policy when they installed Chiang Kai-shek's representatives there after Japan's surrender. But the Generalissimo's men treated Formosa as a conquered province and set about establishing a new overlordship. Those who objected were suppressed by whatever means necessary, or by whatever means happened to please the agents of the Kuomintang. When the struggle went badly for Chiang on the mainland, he evacuated his government to the island and set up a "temporary" regime in Taipei. The "loss" of China caused an uproar in American politics, with Republicans seizing upon the issue to condemn (in ascending order, and with appropriate crescendo): disloyal foreign service officers for recommending that Chiang's government be left to its fate; the so-called "containment" policy for neglecting Asia; Secretary of State Dean Acheson on general principles; and all Democrats collectively for allowing it to happen.

Disgusted with Chiang's repressive warlords, and perhaps seeking to leave the door open to adjustment with the new communist regime in China, Truman had declared that American military forces would not intervene to protect the rump government on Formosa. But the furor did not die; clearly the Republicans believed they were on to something big. Many were appalled when Senator Joseph R. McCarthy tried to exploit the China issue in crude fashion, but the administration's Cold War rhetoric had given him the opportunity to convert the broad attack on communists in government into the dominant theme it became. Against this background of events, Truman declared a new China policy in his June 27 message on Korea: the Seventh Fleet was ordered to prevent any attack on Formosa. The fleet would also prevent attacks in the other direction, from the island to the mainland, but the primary effect of Truman's order was to place the island under American military protection until its future status could be determined, sometime after "the restoration of security in the Pacific." How long that would take depended upon several conditions, not the least of which would be the political climate in the United States.

Truman's hypothesis on the origins of the Korean War—that it had begun because the Soviet Union had abandoned subversion in favor of armed conquest—and his decision to move the Seventh Fleet into the Formosan straits, opened the way for increased agitation by those who wished to defend Chiang by aiding South Korea, and who prayed for the day when, as comrades in arms, Americans and Chinese Nationalists would return to the mainland. The President may have hoped to quiet the "China Lobby" and to prevent Chiang from expanding the war on his own, but the results of his actions were quite different. Meanwhile, the American (and UN) commander in the Far East, General Douglas MacArthur, ordered three squadrons of jet fighters to Formosa.

The Philippines presented a different sort of dilemma. Granted independence on July 4, 1946, the islands had already developed serious internal problems. President Manuel Roxas, a leading member of the group that had played both sides of the street during the Japanese occupation, had made his first order of business the suppression of the peasant guerrilla movement which had provided the main resistance to the Japanese occupation. Like Greek and Italian partisans, the Philippine guerrillas had developed a set of political aims incompatible with the goals of the restoration. Organized under the name of Hukbalahap, they seized power in rural villages, took over the land, and set up local communes. Roxas's efforts to quash the movement in its infancy were unsuccessful. By 1950 even the roads in and out of Manila were unsafe at night, and the "Huks" were staging bold raids on the truck convoys that had been organized to keep the city supplied. American observers had watched these events with growing despair. Once Truman established that "communism" had passed beyond subversion to military conquest, he could justify, as he did in the June 27 speech, an increase in United States forces in the Philippines and stepped-up military assistance. Although nominally independent, the Philippines became a military protectorate in the shadow of the Korean War.

Truman sent as special adviser to the Philippines Colonel Edward Lansdale, an expert in the techniques of what would soon be called "counter-insurgency" warfare. President Dwight D. Eisenhower later transferred Lansdale from the Philippines to Indochina, thus beginning what would eventually become America's longest war. Lansdale and the Korean War are both critical reference points in tracing the history of American involvement in Asia. Washington had puzzled over what to do about Indochina ever since the beginning of World War II. Franklin D. Roosevelt had given serious thought to putting the area under a United Nations trusteeship; he was determined that the area should not be handed back to the French. Yet as the war in Europe neared an end, Roosevelt wavered on this (and other) postwar questions. Truman helped the French to reoccupy Saigon and Hanoi, but with little enthusiasm, and with even less faith in France's ability to overcome the Vietminh movement headed by Ho Chi-minh. In the immediate postwar period, American policy toward Indochina was in the doldrums: unhappy with the French colonialist policy, but increasingly afraid of the political success of Ho, a declared Marxist with ties to Moscow. Early in 1947 the State Department confessed that it had no answer to the dilemma.

From that point on, the United States backed into an unstated, indirect policy of helping the French to restore full control over their rebellious colony, in part because Washington desired Paris's support on European questions, and in part simply because it could not prevent the French from diverting Marshall Plan or NATO aid to the war in Indochina. Then, after Chiang's defeat and Peking's and Moscow's recognition of Ho Chi-minh's Democratic Republic of Vietnam, the United States granted the French puppet ruler Bao Dai formal recognition and thereby assured his international legitimacy. Secretary of State Acheson put it this way in a

February 16, 1950, memorandum to Truman: "The choice confronting the U.S. is to support the legal governments in Indochina or to face the extension of Communism over the remainder of the continental area of Southeast Asia and possibly westward." Less than two months before the outbreak of the Korean War, the United States promised economic and military aid to the French in Indochina, beginning with a grant of $10 million. Truman converted this tentative step into firm policy in the June 27 speech: "I have . . . directed acceleration in the furnishing of military assistance to the forces of France and the Associated States in Indo-china and the dispatch of a military mission to provide close working relations with those forces."

Unnoticed by most of his listeners, whose attention was fastened on the unfolding events in Korea itself, the President had set a new course in Asia. The full consequences of his policies toward Formosa, the Philippines, and Indochina still could not be grasped when the Korean War ended in 1953. Policies begun during the Korean War would also have long-range effects in (and on) Japan and Germany. Special Ambassador John Foster Dulles was in Japan consulting with General MacArthur about the outlines of a peace treaty with that World War II foe when word came of the Korean invasion. Dulles at once cabled the State Department to urge that all necessary action be taken to defend the South Korean government. In Japan Dulles had observed a growing "neutralist" temper among the nation's leaders; MacArthur had warned that the United States was running out of time in Japan. But neither man had an answer for the seemingly insurmountable problems involved in writing a peace treaty designed to keep this industrial power on the right side in the Cold War.

China's shift to communism had almost finished American hopes that Japan could remain independent economically, and if that were indeed impossible, then a political defection was only a matter of time. Any peace treaty would have to confront the China problem at once: Who would sign for China, Peking or Taipei? Who was entitled to reparations, the mainland government or the "temporary" capital on Formosa? And who was the legitimate heir to Formosa itself? There seemed no way to prevent the re-establishment of close contacts between Japan and mainland China. When the Korean War began, the peace treaty issue took on a new complexion. At first some policy-makers thought it offered a badly needed reason to postpone action; but this idea gave way to the rapidly dawning realization that with Communist China in at least a semi-adversary position, there might never be a better time to complete the treaty!

Japan's brief flirtation with "neutrality" was brought to a sudden end by the men who sent Japan-based American airplanes against Korea. Japan became an American "privileged sanctuary," and by the military bilateral agreement signed at the time of the peace treaty on September 7, 1951, that status was confirmed for ten more years. Japan thus moved (or was moved) into the "Free World" via Korea. Both treaties were signed over Russia's protests, but *neither* China had anything to say about the terms of Japan's re-entry into world politics. Without the Korean War, United States policy-makers probably could not have ignored the wishes of either Chinese government, nor so easily have persuaded its Allies to go along with a "generous" approach to the Japanese peace treaty.

MacArthur had pointed out to Dulles, and anyone else willing to listen, that America's position in Japan was quite different from the situation in Germany, where four powers shared responsibility for the occupation—and could blame one another for whatever hardships the Germans suffered. But if that were so, it was also true that no matter what happened in Korea there was no chance for an all-German peace treaty on the Japanese pattern. The United States had settled for the establishment of a West German government at Bonn; but the Defense Department insisted that Europe could not be defended without West German participation in NATO. While State Department officials had their own reasons for wanting German integration on all levels, the United States government's public position was still that the only possible solution to the "problem" was demilitarization. Secretary Acheson had restated this policy as recently as June 5, 1950. Objections to

German rearmament were strongest in France, but other NATO members were less than enthusiastic about the possibility. Congress had not welcomed arguments in that direction.

As "United Nations" forces were being driven back toward the Pusan perimeter in the southeast corner of Korea, Secretary of State Acheson delivered a solemn warning: "It is now clear to all —if indeed it was not clear before—that free nations must be united, they must be determined, and they must be strong, if they are to preserve their freedom and maintain a righteous peace. There is no other way." America's European allies learned what this would entail on September 12, 1950, when Acheson told the British and French Foreign Ministers that the United States proposed to create ten German divisions for NATO. The United States, of course, would ask its own citizens to bear the costs of massive rearmament; it was only fair that Europeans pay their share and accept the hard fact that one way or another Germany would be rearmed.

Three days later General MacArthur broke out of the Pusan perimeter with a brilliant amphibious landing at Inchon, behind North Korean lines. His advance was as fast as the retreat had been, even faster it seemed. The General was soon perched on the 38th parallel, asking permission to cross and destroy what remained of the invading force and, by implication, the North Korean government. Pyongyang was about to be the first satellite capital "liberated" by UN forces.

Thus far we have seen that American policy-makers regarded the Korean War as a broad challenge, and responded with equally far-reaching decisions which covered a list of troublesome problems. It is clear, moreover, that these other Asian (and European) problems influenced policy-makers' perceptions of the Korean situation, and dictated a firm stand against communist expansion. From September 1950 until the truce in July 1953, military developments in Korea came to dictate larger policy decisions, reversing the previous order of things as the war changed from a war of containment to a war of liberation, and finally to a prolonged test of wills. In understanding events in Korea after MacArthur's drive to the 38th parallel, some earlier history is essential.

In the 1943 Cairo Declaration, the Big Three had promised that "in due course Korea shall become free and independent." Held in subjection by Japan since 1910, Korea had a long history of previous occupations and rule from foreign capitals. American interest in an "independent" Korea developed in the period following the American Civil War, at a time when plans for a general commercial campaign in the Pacific were being laid. But after some desultory efforts to open the "Hermit Kingdom" to the outside world, as Perry had opened Japan in 1852, the United States allowed Korea to disappear behind Japan's suzerainty following the Russo-Japanese War. Actually, there was not much America could have done about Korea even if it had wanted to raise a fuss about the matter. What the State Department sought instead, therefore, was to extract some sort of pledge from the Japanese concerning the Philippine Islands as the price for not raising the Korean question.

During World War II, President Roosevelt and his advisers thought it might take twenty to thirty years of trusteeship before Korea was ready for complete independence. The dropping of the atomic bomb, which forced Japan's sudden decision to surrender, likewise forced precipitate decisions by its conquerors. One of these was the decision that Russian commanders should accept the surrender of Japanese troops above the 38th parallel in Korea, while American commanders would accept surrenders below that line. Almost immediately, however, General John R. Hodge ran into political difficulties in the South. His efforts to achieve a gradual transfer of power to Korean civil authorities brought a storm of protest from nationalist political leaders who wanted the immediate eradication of the last vestiges of Japan's forty-year rule. Hodge agreed to this demand, but he would not recognize any provisional Korean government. New Russian-American talks in December 1945 led to a big-power effort to impose a five-year trusteeship on all of Korea, but when discussions were initiated with Korean political leaders the following March, the Soviets refused to talk with those who opposed the trusteeship. Since none of the political parties in the South was willing to accept the trusteeship plan, except the Communists, American officials were left in an embarrassing position. They were unable to carry out their own plan without alienating non-Communists, and perhaps turning Korea over to potentially unfriendly hands for a second time.

President Truman sent a special emissary, Edwin W. Pauley, to Korea in June 1946. Pauley was alarmed by what he saw. Allowed to travel in North Korea by Soviet authorities, he found that they were not removing capital equipment as in Eastern Europe and Manchuria, but were seeking to replace the broken economic lines to Japan with new ties to the Soviet Union. Korea, he asserted, was "an ideological battleground upon which our entire success in Asia may depend." Lacking an all-Korean solution, officials on both sides of the parallel moved to establish dependable governments for the interim, however long that might last. Meanwhile, the Soviets began a military withdrawal which, by the end of the summer, had removed all but ten thousand of their troops. American forces also began planning for withdrawal. But each side was troubled by what it was leaving behind. In early 1947 General Hodge reported to President Truman that the stage was being set for a Korean civil war unless Russian-American cooperation could head off the conflict. Another round of talks with the Russians produced no agreement, since they still insisted upon the trusteeship solution. Unable to move South Korean political leaders, and unwilling to accept a Russian counterproposal of total withdrawal from both "Koreas," the United States took the question to the UN General Assembly.

There the United States proposed that UN-supervised elections be held in each area as a first step toward the formation of a national government. The Russians objected to the whole procedure, first to last, and charged that the United States had violated the 1945 Moscow Agreement by taking the issue to the United Nations. The Russians' real concern here was not Korea but the precedent for settling the fate of wartime issues in the world organization. They were especially concerned about Germany at this moment, as the Berlin blockade would soon demonstrate in dramatic fashion. If the division of Korea could be settled by the UN, so could a German settlement be imposed by UN mandate forced through by the United States and its supporters.

The United States went ahead with elections below the parallel under UN auspices. These were certified as a "valid expression of the free will of the electorate" in those parts of Korea accessible to the UN commission sent to observe the elections—areas which contained approximately two-thirds of the Korean people. A constitution was written by the newly elected "National Assembly," and Syngman Rhee was elected the first president of the Republic of Korea. A stipulated number of seats were left for Northern representatives whenever they decided to join this rightful government and swear allegiance to its constitution.

Having established a government with international status, Truman felt he could withdraw remaining American forces with some sense of security about what he was leaving in their place. The Joint Chiefs had urged an end to the occupation of South Korea on several grounds, including, as a final argument, their fear that lack of progress toward a unified Korea would eventually produce "violent disorder," which would make the American position untenable. If the nation's military forces were obliged to retreat hastily, the United States would suffer a loss of prestige, "quite possibly to the extent of adversely affecting cooperation in other areas more vital to the security" of the country.

Whatever doubts military spokesmen continued to have about the Korean situation after the UN-sponsored elections, the President and his political advisers apparently felt they had come up with a fairly good solution. But South Korea did not prosper, economically or politically. Economically, the 38th parallel cut across agricultural and industrial lifelines, leaving North and South to suffer serious deprivations as a consequence of big-power desires for a finite dividing line between their spheres of influence. Politically, Syngman Rhee started out on the path trod by Chiang Kaishek, relying upon conservatives and reactionaries to maintain himself in power, and employing repressive measures against all opponents. By early 1950 his regime had become something of a liability to the United States. Kim Il-sung's position in Pyongyang was somewhat more protected, but he liked the division of Korea no more than the aged leader who ruled in Seoul. Kim did not have a Secretary Acheson carping at him about holding free elections; and he was getting Russian tanks. Rhee had been warned that unless newly scheduled parliamentary elections were held there would be no more American aid; and he had been informed that he was not getting tanks or any other equipment needed to carry out his oft-repeated pledge to unite the peninsula.

The administration's determination to discourage Rhee's adventurism may help to account for Acheson's ambiguity in a January 1950 speech which redefined America's strategic defense perimeters. In the first part of the speech he left Korea outside of those lines, but then went on to assure countries in this position that they could rely upon the United Nations for support—if they were attacked by an aggressor. This way Rhee (or other ambitious "allies") could not drag the United States into unwanted conflicts. This explanation of Acheson's intent jibes with an event which occurred exactly one week before the North Korean military advance. In remarks cleared by Acheson, Special Ambassador John Foster Dulles assured the members of the Korean "National Assembly" in Seoul, "You are not alone . . . so long as you continue to play worthily your part in the great design of human freedom."

For several months before Dulles's appearance in Seoul, reports of a North Korean buildup had been featured in American intelligence briefings. Sometimes an attack date was specified. But these reports were discounted by analysts who had to screen similar reports from practically every front line in the Cold War. They had become accustomed to strong rhetoric on both sides of the 38th parallel, and even to the constant pinprick attacks back and forth across the dividing line. Russia's role in these pre-invasion maneuvers, and in the actual invasion, remains unclear. Nikita Khrushchev's purported "Memoirs" insist that Stalin's role was confined to approving a plan presented by an eager Kim Il-sung.

Secondary accounts published in the United States "assume" that the Soviet Union planned the attack, perhaps encouraged unwittingly by Acheson himself when he placed South Korea outside the strategic defense perimeter. There is no consensus, however, when it comes to the question of larger motivations lurking behind the decision to go ahead with the attack. Recent writers, including a few of America's most prestigious Cold Warriors, have suggested that if Secretary Acheson did not regard Korea as falling within America's defense perimeters, the Soviets certainly considered it within their own and acted accordingly when the United States moved unilaterally to make peace in Japan. The author of the "containment" policy, George F. Kennan, has written that it occurred to him at the time that there might have been a "connection" between Washington's decision to proceed independently with a Japanese peace settlement, including a long-term American military presence there, and the Russian decision "to unleash a civil war in Korea."

In another category of interpretation is I. F. Stone's *Hidden History of the Korean War*. Stone was alone in 1952 in arguing that Rhee had started the war, or else deliberately provoked a massive attack as the only way to save his tottering regime by bringing America into a local conflict. Relying almost exclusively on the pro-war *New York Times,* Stone proceeded to lay out the case against Truman's "intervention" from its own reporters' words and to paint a sinister portrait of General MacArthur's desire to make the Korean War into a Far Eastern "Sarajevo" for war against China. When one adjusts for these extremes, Stone's book remains an impressive critique of American policy in the first eighteen months of the war. It was reprinted in 1969, at the height of national concern over the unending agony of the Vietnam War, but neither Stone's sweeping indictment of American policies nor the more cautious suggestions of Cold War "realists" have yet replaced the original interpretation of the Korean War as a clear-cut case of Russian aggression.

There has been, on the other hand, almost no dissent from the view that General MacArthur's military tactics after crossing the

38th parallel were unnecessarily provocative and contributed greatly to the Chinese decision to intervene in the war. It suited the administration's needs to saddle the general with full responsibility for the debacle which began when Chinese troops came pouring across the Yalu River at the end of November 1950 to halt his drive to the Manchurian border. It also suited the administration's purposes, however, to have China branded as an aggressor by the United Nations for launching this counterattack in the face of American determination to replace the North Korean government with a pro-American all-Korean regime headed by Syngman Rhee. The Democratic leadership managed to have it both ways: they could blame MacArthur for military errors and political failings while satisfying conservative critics by having China denounced before the world organization.

When MacArthur reached the 38th parallel following the Inchon landing, there were sound political and military reasons for halting his army on that line. There were equally powerful reasons, primarily psychological and ideological, for not doing so. Some policy-makers later admitted that they feared MacArthur's prestige; others feared what would happen to congressional and allied support for Cold War policies if the General were prevented from completing the "liberation" of North Korea. After calculating all the risks involved in crossing (and not crossing) the parallel, the administration gave MacArthur a go-ahead for his plan but instructed him not to make a public statement on the crossing. He was further told to report on Soviet or Chinese intervention before engaging such forces. Whatever blunders MacArthur would make in the future, the basic political decision to unite Korea by force was not a usurpation by an ambitious general in the field but an agreed-upon goal set forth in detailed instructions.

As an added precaution against Chinese intervention, MacArthur was told to use only Republic of Korea forces as he approached the northernmost parts of the peninsula. Meanwhile, Secretary of State Acheson publicly reassured Peking that the United States had no aggressive designs upon Chinese territory. Had he been engaged in dealings with what Americans liked to call "traditional" China, these somewhat condescending efforts to inform China's leaders of America's intentions might have been of some value. But he was not, and they were not.

Truman's meeting with MacArthur on Wake Island on October 15, 1950, was supposed to be a personal follow-up to Washington's precautionary instructions. Instead it became a victory celebration. Discussion soon turned to the postwar Korean government. The problem would be, said Assistant Secretary of State Dean Rusk, who had accompanied the President to the conference, that "there has been an effective propaganda campaign against the Rhee government" in the United Nations. Truman and MacArthur put aside such complaints, agreeing that, in the President's words, "We must make it plain that we are supporting the Rhee government and propaganda can go to hell." Plans were laid for using South Korean civilian officials to re-establish local government in the North and to supervise local elections. At Wake Island, in short, the stated goal of the United Nations, the reunification of Korea, was subordinated by American leaders to the protection of the Rhee government.

The Wake Island conference is most remembered, however, for General MacArthur's predictions that the Chinese Communists would not intervene and that the war would be all but over by Christmas. He even told the President that some of his troops could be withdrawn for European duties in early 1951. Along with the rest of the nation, the *New York Times* relaxed editorially: "Except for unexpected developments along the frontiers of the peninsula, we can now be easy in our minds as to the military outcome." MacArthur launched his final drive to the borders in late October, removing on his own initiative the Joint Chiefs' restrictions on the use of non-Korean troops close to the Manchurian frontier. When he was questioned about this decision, MacArthur insisted the Republic of Korea troops could not do it all by themselves, adding somewhat cryptically that the subject had been covered at Wake Island.

In the near euphoria prevailing in these post-Inchon weeks, when the momentum of Asian events seemed to be flowing with

MacArthur, few thought it worthwhile to pursue the matter of troop deployments. Then, suddenly, the Chinese Communists began marching into Korea across the bridges over the Yalu River. The Indian government had transmitted Chou En-lai's prior warnings to the State Department, but Secretary Acheson's public evaluation of these was, "I should think it would be sheer madness on the part of the Chinese Communists to do that." Yet the administration was not now inclined to listen to MacArthur's recommendations for dealing with this "madness" even when it seemed that his forces might not be able to hold the peninsula. By March 1951 the battlelines were again drawn around the 38th parallel, but MacArthur wanted to use the Chinese Communist intervention as justification for an all-out effort to "neutralize China's capability to wage aggressive war and thus save Asia from the engulfment otherwise facing it." Sobered by the experiences of land warfare against the quilt-uniformed Chinese, and convinced that to enlarge the struggle in Korea would be the wrong war, at the wrong place, at the wrong time, against the wrong enemy, American policy-makers reluctantly accepted the only alternative: reestablishment of a divided Korea.

MacArthur would not: his insistence upon seeking allies in the Republican leadership in Congress, his habit of publicizing disagreements with the Pentagon, and his purposeful effort to undermine the initiation of truce negotiations in April 1951 brought Truman to the painful decision to remove the General. It was painful not because of a close personal bond between the two men, but because MacArthur was the only popular hero in what had become an extremely unpopular war. Truman's own popularity sank to new lows after the General's recall. MacArthur used every opportunity to drive it still lower; he was greeted as a returning hero in each of the cities he visited—San Francisco, Chicago, New York (where twice the number of people lined the streets to see him as had honored Eisenhower on his return from the Crusade in Europe), Boston, and, finally, Washington. Before a joint session of Congress, MacArthur delivered an emotional "Farewell Address" in defense of his conduct of the war. The message was carried over a nationwide radio network into every community, and often into every school in the community. Within days of this appearance, his words were being marketed on long-playing records. And the popular singer Vaughn Monroe capitalized on the General's concluding quotation of an old army ballad, "Old Soldiers Never Die," to record a new "hit song."

Congress conducted a full-scale investigation of the General's removal, and extended it to include a review of Far Eastern policy since 1945, but MacArthur's role as his own star witness brought him back down to earth with other mortals. Herbert Hoover still saw in him "a reincarnation of St. Paul into a great General of the Army who came out of the East," but his star was on the wane. It faded out ingloriously after a last brief flare at the 1952 Republican national convention. The plain and simple fact was that not even MacArthur's staunchest supporters could go along with his recommendations for carrying the war to China, except in flights of political fancy and rhetoric. Along with many others in both parties, they were determined only to prevent the Truman administration from making MacArthur the sole scapegoat for a gamut of unwise political and tactical decisions. A greater opportunity was at hand: the nomination of another hero, General Dwight D. Eisenhower, who would appeal to a voting public disenchanted with the war, and whose record for "winning" might even survive a compromise settlement to extricate the nation from the Korean imbroglio.

Truce talks had been under way for more than a year when Eisenhower was nominated by the Republicans in the summer of 1952. They had stalled on several issues, including the future demarcation line, the matter of postwar bases in both North and South Korea, and, most difficult of all, the prisoner-of-war question. The North Koreans and Chinese demanded immediate repatriation of all POW's; the United States and its allies insisted that those who wished not to return to communist-dominated lands be permitted to remain in South Korea. It was a typical Cold War dilemma, with each side anxious not to miss the slightest opportunity to embarrass the other. MacArthur's successor, General

Matthew Ridgway, had instructed his negotiators at the outset of the truce negotiations to be firm on all issues, so that "history may record that Communist military aggression reached its high water mark in Korea, and that thereafter Communism itself began its recession in Asia."

The notion that a "victorious" settlement would produce a general retreat by "communism" throughout Asia was of questionable value as a premise for negotiations leading to a way out of a bad situation. Eisenhower quite rightly ignored it. During the 1952 campaign he pledged to "Go to Korea" to assess the situation in person. Military commanders in Korea drew up impressive plans for new tactical offensives to persuade the communists to negotiate better terms, but Eisenhower ignored these too, much to the surprise and chagrin of some of his old comrades in arms.

Upon his return to the United States, Eisenhower warned that a prolonged delay in the negotiations would be intolerable. In the following weeks he combined additional warnings and veiled threats to use atomic weapons if full-scale fighting erupted again, with assurances that the United States sought an honorable armistice in Korea. In one notable speech on April 16, 1953, Eisenhower offered to discuss a wide range of issues with the communists once the fighting ended. His military credibility enhanced the force of any atomic threat, however veiled; his prestige allowed him a free hand with friends and foes, at home and abroad. A compromise on the POW issue was found, one which permitted each side to save face by turning the problem of repatriation over to a committee of neutral nations. But, when all is said and done, the difference between Truman and Eisenhower, the difference which made it possible for the latter to negotiate a Korean truce, was that the political costs were too high to allow Truman to make peace without victory, and too high to allow Eisenhower to make war without seeking peace.

Secretary of the Treasury George M. Humphrey summed up the new administration's feelings about Korea in an early Cabinet meeting: "You *have* to get Korea *out of the way*." The trick was to induce the other side to settle on the compromise terms by holding up both the irrational and the rational solutions. Both these options were closed to the Truman administration, by now a prisoner of its critics and of its own Cold War rhetoric. Eisenhower was perhaps the only man in the country who could have taken the nation out of the Korean War on the terms that he did without surrendering, or even modifying, the basic premises of America's larger Cold War policies. His Secretary of State, John Foster Dulles, insisted that the new administration's foreign policy was as different from "containment" as day from night. But however he defined it, "liberation" would come down to the same thing. Korea had been a mistake, or at least badly mishandled. In the future other ways would have to be found to check the growing menace of Asian communism. When Dulles and his aides developed these new methods, they still depended upon assumptions held by him and others at the beginning of the Korean War.

Until now few questions have been raised about this almost forgotten "police action," yet the Korean War set the stage for what was to come later in Southeast Asia. It began the era of gigantic military budgets; it confirmed and increased the power of the presidency in foreign affairs; and it defined the world in a way which put the United States at odds with revolutionary nationalism, as well as with "communism" anywhere.

Part 1

SETTING FOR A "LIMITED WAR"

AS THE FIRST article in this section declares, the "China Crisis" had become, by the end of 1948, a crisis for "Us," that is, for traditional American foreign policy. Whereas the occupation of Eastern Europe by the Soviet Union could be discounted as an unfortunate result of World War II, communist gains in Asia were of a far different order. The impact of Mao Tse-tung's impending victory in the Chinese Civil War was all the greater because Americans had serenely assumed that China, accorded equal status in the "Big Four" by Franklin Roosevelt, would become the principal stabilizing power in postwar Asia. Nathaniel Peffer's blunt assertion that the only thing certain about China was that the "Generalissimo's government is tottering" was hardly front-page news in November 1948; his discussion of the alternatives facing policymakers shows how up in the air American policy was.

First surveys of Asia after the dust settled in China were hardly optimistic: the range of choices in the Far East had seemingly narrowed to what Henry R. Lieberman described as "mixed parliamentary socialism" on the Indian model, and "mixed Communist-sponsored socialism" like that professed by the new rulers in Peking. Neither appealed to Washington. China's defection (for that is what American policy-makers seemed to think the Communist victory amounted to), spurred efforts to shore up remaining Asian ramparts to contain Soviet expansionism. Okinawa was already being converted into a strategic bomber base, capable of sending atomic weapons against either China or Russia. No doubt this generous investment of congressional funds on behalf of the Strategic Air Command impressed communist military leaders in both countries, though, as we have seen, surprisingly little attention has been paid to a possible connection between America's growing foothold in Asia and the presumed Soviet desire to encourage Kim Il-sung's plan to end the division of Korea and thus eliminate a potential danger there. More important to both sides, certainly, was future American policy in Japan. *Times* staff writer Lindesay Parrott summarized the "touchy issue" of a peace treaty with Japan, concluding that it was almost impossible to write a treaty that would allow Tokyo to avoid "standing up and being counted on one side or the other."

British Russian expert Edward Crankshaw's critique of the "containment" policy was typical of the argument used to justify American intervention in the Korean War. The only real danger of a general war with the Soviet Union, Crankshaw suggested, stemmed from the possibility that the West might grow tired of maintaining a state of preparedness, giving the Soviets a false impression of how far they could go. This situation was likely to lead to a Western ultimatum and a general war neither side really wanted: ". . . If our statesmen can bring themselves to think aggressively instead of defensively, then there is every chance that we shall be able to do without an ultimatum at all." Crankshaw's reasoned arguments are a good corrective to the notion that Truman's decision to go into Korea was primarily determined by the need to satisfy Republican critics. Crankshaw (and others) had spotted key weaknesses in the "containment" policy (and mentality). These weaknesses suggest that future studies of America in the Korean War will have to consider that the decision to intervene was determined by a need to re-establish the credibility of the "containment" policy on a higher level, and, indeed, the credibility of the atomic deterrent. If the greatest exercise of power is in fact knowing how and where to practice restraint, the Truman administration may have seized upon limited war as the only way to prove American intentions.

John Foster Dulles makes these very points in the article which completes this first section, adding, as had earlier American statesmen at the turn of the century, that the war would have the important effect of lifting the nation out of purposeless materialism.

The China Crisis
Is a Crisis for Us

by Nathaniel Peffer

MANCHURIA HAS FALLEN to the Chinese Communists. All of North China must almost inevitably follow. That the Chiang Kai-shek government can long stand as the national government of China is almost inconceivable. More is involved, however, than victory and defeat in a Far Eastern civil war. The world's political balance has tipped and, moreover, tipped in a direction opposite to that which America had hoped for. The effect on the order of world politics and on America is profound, and for America the necessity has arisen for a difficult and, it may be, historic decision.

The two salient facts are, first, that China is now being drawn into the Communist orbit and, second, that America, since it has been supporting, even underwriting, the Chiang Kai-shek government, has suffered a severe reverse. In consequence America must decide whether to accept the reverse and write off the loss, or try to arrest further drift into the Communist orbit, however great the risk entailed.

The question now is whether a country with one-fifth of the

From the *New York Times Magazine,* November 14, 1938, copyright © 1938, 1966 by The New York Times Company.

world's population and one of the largest land masses of the globe is to become a satellite of Moscow, at Moscow's disposal politically, as are Poland, Rumania, Bulgaria and Hungary, and perhaps at Moscow's disposal, too, for military purposes. America must choose between waiting to see if the danger materializes into reality, and taking appropriate action now to forestall it.

This necessity for choice is not new. It is not wholly the result of the disaster to Nanking's arms in the last two weeks. Nanking's apparently sensational defeats have only given it dramatic accent. To those with any experience in China it has long been obvious that Manchuria would fall and that North China could not be held.

But because the process of the Nanking government's deterioration was slow, though steady, it was possible for America to evade clear decision, to continue neither getting out nor getting in, to postpone unpleasant choice by throwing Nationalist China periodic "sops" in the form of financial "aid," enough to keep it from collapsing at the moment and not enough to give it something on which to stand. The amount at any one time was small but the total exceeds two billion dollars, and China is worse off than at the beginning.

Now the cumulative effect of deterioration has begun to tell. The foundation, sapped little by little over a long time, is suddenly giving way. The Chinese are not particularly shocked, having expected it for a long time and discounted it. America, however, is shocked. And in a sense the Chinese government's débâcle is not an unmixed evil for America. It presents an issue that can no longer be dodged.

What will happen in China no one can foretell in detail, but the general direction is unmistakable. The one certainty is that the Chiang Kai-shek government is tottering. Unless shored up from without—and this means buttressing on a scale not yet attempted or even considered—it will fall or at best survive as a small local regime, carrying perhaps international recognition but exercising no authority outside its immediate environs. This, too, will surprise Chinese less than Americans. A plebiscite a year ago of the hundreds of Chinese students attending American colleges would have shown a large majority believing that the Nationalist government would not last two years.

What will succeed the Nationalist government is not so clear. There may be a coalition, but a coalition in name only. Two years ago, when General Marshall was striving for a genuine settlement, there might have been a genuine coalition, that is, a government representing all parties and schools of opinion. But at first the Nationalist government would have none of it and later, when the Nationalist government began to sag, the Communists saw no advantage in it. Today, a coalition government would be a Communist government with a few non-Communists for decorative effect. For practical purposes, whatever the official government, the Communists will soon exercise power over at least half the country and before long quite likely over the whole country.

This has an internal and an external aspect. The internal is the less serious. So far as the rest of the world is concerned it is mainly a matter of philosophical interest whether the Chinese order their economic affairs on a collectivist principle or an Adam Smith principle, so long as the Chinese alone are affected.

What matters to the rest of the world is whether China is arrayed in a coalition which is a power bloc as well as an exemplar of a social philosophy. In a few words, what matters is whether China will become another satellite of Russia or at least an arm of Russian foreign policy.

Which it will be no one who is free from prejudice can answer now with certainty. One can, as a matter of fact, be more confident that China will not be a Communist society at the outset than that it will not be a Russian satellite. The Chinese Communists have long made their program known, and there is no reason to disbelieve them, since it is not calculated to win them friends in the non-Communist world. For one thing, they repudiate the pleasant notions once circulated in this country that they were only agrarian reformers. They admit bluntly and without pressing that they are Marxists and that their aim is a Marxist society in China.

But the Communists know that China, as an unindustrialized country lacking in technological experience and surplus capital, must go through several transitional phases before it can arrive at genuine communization. These phases include a fairly high degree of private ownership and management and a degree of political democracy. There would be a mixed economy, with both state ownership and private ownership in smaller enterprises and there would be for a time representative political institutions.

On the external aspect there is more cause for doubt and concern. The Communist leaders maintain or used to maintain that while they have a philosophical affinity with Russia, their role in world affairs would be Chinese and autonomous. This thesis becomes acceptable only with reservations now that America has armed and subsidized their enemies, and now that the Russian-American cleavage cuts across the whole world.

Yet there are still some grounds for believing that the Chinese Communists would remain their own masters. In this connection the Tito episode may be significant. In so far as Serb nationalism has played a part in Yugoslav intransigence, there is reason for hope from a Communist China. Chinese nationalism is as self-conscious as Serb nationalism. There is in China no element of instinctive kinship with Russia such as the Serbs feel as Slavs. On the contrary, there is an instinctive suspicion of all white powers.

Further, the Chinese Communist party has been established long enough and was cut off from Russia long enough to have become nationalized in a way that no other Communist party is outside Russia. The Chinese Communist leaders have worked out their own methods, their own theories, their own program for nearly thirty years; it is far from certain that when finally successful after a long struggle they will immediately surrender control of their own movement.

More important, the success of communism in China is conditional on industrialization and modernization, which in turn are conditional on capital goods obtained on credit, which in turn can come only from America. There would thus be some reason for not antagonizing America by too close an affiliation with Russia.

Against all this, however, is the fact that the propaganda of the Chinese Communists in the last two years has been in exact harmony with that of Russia. It has become more virulently anti-American as Russian-American relations have worsened. While it is true that American help for Chiang Kai-shek has given the Communists a grievance of their own, it is also true that in content, direction and intensity, their propaganda has more closely reflected America's relations with Russia than America's relations with China. And if the division of the world into two camps becomes sharper, there is at the very least a fair presumption that the Chinese Communists will conclude that no country can stay neutral and that therefore China must array itself with Russia.

In that case the consequences for all of Eastern Asia would be fateful. Russia would hold sway from the Adriatic to the Pacific. American prestige would be one of the victims. Whatever the reason may have been—whether in anticipation of China's economic potentialities when industrially developed or in fear of threat from a strong power established on the opposite shore of the Pacific or just in reluctance to abandon a diplomatic position once taken—the fact is that America has for decades assumed the role of sponsor and guarantor of China's sovereignty. Thus, national prestige is involved, and at a time when the world is apparently dividing into two camps and prestige is not only a token but a political weapon.

China has been and is the magnetic center of Eastern Asia, drawing to itself all that lies around and beyond it with almost polar force. It is difficult to conceive of China being attached to Russia even after the manner of the Balkans, without the rest of Eastern Asia, if not all Asia, following after it as if pulled by gravitation.

Economically Eastern Asia at least would be sequestered from the rest of the world. It would be for Russia to develop its resources, to transmute them into military potential and then to confront the Western world with a Eurasia integrated for whatever purpose Moscow elected. It would be the most powerful empire known to man, the Roman and British not excepted.

What must we in America do? One thing is now beyond argument: the course followed up to the present has been futile. To continue it would be dangerous as well as futile. Doling out money to Chiang Kai-shek is useless. Money will not keep his Government from falling. Neither will arms. As a matter of fact the Chinese Communists now are fighting with American arms they have captured from the Nationalists, and the more arms we send Chiang Kai-shek the more the Communists will have.

Military "advisers" to train Chinese soldiers for efficiency in the future are equally useless. The Chinese armies now in being will be wiped out or captured before then.

The inescapable fact is that the Nationalist armies are irrecoverably beaten and must be written off. And the Nanking government cannot survive by its own efforts alone or by its own efforts reinforced by America.

America can no longer temporize or postpone choice by resort to financial driblets. One of two things must be done, and the effectiveness of either will be in proportion to the expeditiousness with which it is done. Either China must be written off or America must intervene in full force. Let us consider the cases for each alternative.

The first choice means acceptance of Communist rule over China, with the probability that China will then adhere to the Russian bloc. In that case America must count on one of two things: either that there will be a general settlement with Russia on a world-wide basis or that, if conflict is inescapable, America will seek decision in the West rather than in Asia. This means, of course, letting Asia go to Russia by default in advance.

If that risk is deemed too great—and a good case can be made for such a position—then the only other course is to interdict Communist control over China and to take effective measures to that end. That means sending in a large force of American troops with corresponding armament, taking up positions in North China and informing the Communists that they advance further at their peril. It means exercising unofficial but effective control over the Nationalist army, both as to command and organization. It means supervision over the government itself much more closely than in Greece, for example. It means, in short, taking over China until the Communist danger is eliminated or the differences with Russia are settled, with or without war.

That large numbers of the Chinese people would be hostile to such an intervention, including many who are not Communists, is self-evident. But that risk would have to be run. That the Russians might respond in kind, sending their own troops into Manchuria and North China to stiffen up the Communists there, is also possible, if not probable. That risk, too, would have to be run. At any rate the burden of decision would be put on Russia.

But in that way alone can the Nanking government be saved and Communist control over at least half of China frustrated. "Aid," it must again be emphasized, will not serve. It has already aggravated the situation. We have only alienated large groups in China who resent alien intrusion into their affairs for any purpose and who hold us responsible for prolonging the civil war. All there is to show for our efforts now is so much American taxpayers' money thrown away.

What has come about is unfortunate but can no longer be helped. To refuse to face it makes it even worse. A balance of risks has to be drawn and an equation stated. Put otherwise, we have two evils to choose from. We have only to decide which is the lesser. Manifestly that is not easy. Not all the factors are calculable now.

On the most detached appraisal, however, it is difficult to refute the argument that in the event of war with Russia China would be a liability rather than an asset. The Chinese army would be an incubus. The safest course would be to sequester it and to set about training an entirely new one in the expectation that the war would last several years. Meanwhile American forces would have to face a trained, battle-hardened Chinese Communist army in addition to a Russian army. They would be fighting in territory in which at least a large part of the population would be hostile. That the Chinese Communists would be more successful than we in winning adherents among the Chinese populace goes without saying. They are Chinese and we aliens; they are in their own land and they can use the language, as we cannot. The advantages of logistics would be on the Chinese Communist and Russian side, of course. In fact, for America the logistical disadvantages would be almost insuperable.

There is one further objection, less logical but more compelling. It is American public opinion. That the American people could be induced to support a large-scale expedition to China now, at the risk of immediate war, is fanciful, no matter what the rational calculations may be. If this were a dictatorship, it might be managed. But it is not, and the American people have never gone to war on a coolly reasoned intellectual decision when the circumstances did not force decision almost automatically.

Taking both military and political considerations into account, it seems wiser then not to draw the issue with Russia over China. This does not entail complete renunciation. There are positive as well as negative arguments for abstaining. For one thing, it must be repeated that it cannot yet be considered foreordained that the Chinese Communists will resign themselves and their country to Russian jurisdiction. Their revolution has been nationalistic as well as social from the beginning. They may prefer to detach themselves from all coalitions, to retain control over their own destiny and devote themselves first of all to making the country strong, to working out their political and social system in their own way and on their own motive power. They may therefore refuse to attach China as a tail to the Russian kite, to be raised and dropped with the winds of Moscow's foreign policy.

If the worst comes to the worst and the Communists should elect to adhere to the Russian bloc, it will nevertheless take them years to organize the country. It will take them years just to recruit and train enough men for the administrative machinery. It will take them years to solve the agrarian problem and to make a start toward industrialization, without which China's manpower will be the raw material of a military machine and not the finished product.

In the interval there will be time for Russian-American differences to work themselves out one way or the other. Those differences are world-wide and they are therefore susceptible to settlement by compromise on a world basis, one in which China, Japan, Korea and the whole of the Far East will fall naturally into place. If not, and collision proves unavoidable, it would be better for America to take as its main theatre of action one in which we should have allies that can be counted on and where the physical conditions would be less unfavorable to ourselves.

There are, then, three things America can do. One is to continue as it has, frittering away money in the name of aid, which has already proved useless and must be abandoned at once. The other two are to make a forcible intervention in China now, in effect taking over the country, or to do nothing at all and let come what may. Neither is desirable. Neither is without risk. But on balance it is sounder, if only by a process of elimination, to forgo intervention and let events take their course, meanwhile retaining full freedom of action. It will still be open to us to take any measures at any time that developments in the Far East call for, and we can do so then on our own initiative, free of encumbrances and not forced by hostages we have unwittingly given.

Gigantic Questions for Mao —And for Us, Too

by Henry R. Lieberman

OF ALL THE gifts that went to Joseph Stalin on his seventieth birthday, Mao Tze-tung's was probably the most impressive. His pilgrimage to Moscow and his praise of Stalin as the "teacher and friend" of the Chinese people symbolized the developing alliance of the two largest Communist countries on earth. It also served to dispel—at least for the time being—the wishful hopes in the West that Mao Tze-tung might turn out to be an Asiatic Tito.

There was nothing startling about Mao's trip, for he has now been on record for some time as accepting the primacy of Stalin as the world's No. 1 Communist figure. Last July, for example, in his brochure, "On the People's Democratic Dictatorship," he emphasized that China would "lean to one side" and that there was no middle course. He added: "Internationally, we belong to the anti-imperialist front headed by the U.S.S.R., and we can only look for genuinely friendly aid from that front, and not from the imperialist front."

This reference to assistance from the Soviet front suggests that the realistic Mao, confronted with difficult problems at home, coupled his high public praise of Stalin in Moscow with practical, down-to-earth questions in private about what the Russians can now do for the Chinese Communists. Any alliance with China, as the United States has discovered, involves giving as well as receiving. Thus far, the Chinese Communists have contributed far more to world communism than they have received in return.

Once the Communists have completed their mopping-up operations on the Chinese mainland, they will have added close to 450,-000,000 people to the 250,000,000 already living under Communist rule—a total approximating one-third of the world's population. Just as the success of the Russian revolution set Mao Tze-tung to studying Marx, Lenin, Bukharin and Kautsky, so the success of the Chinese Communist revolution is apt to set more young revolutionaries in Asia to studying Mao Tze-tung's "New Democracy."

Throughout the restive, economically backward lands of East Asia, whose nations are confronted with many of the same problems the Communists are tackling in China, Mao Tze-tung's slogans awaken responsive echoes. Thus, just as the Soviet Union exerts a political pull on China, so China exerts a drag of its own on the rest of Asia.

These new conditions, which require an over-all re-examination of our Far Eastern policy in terms of China, the rest of Asia and the world-wide cold war, deserve hard study in the United States. A workable American policy in the Far East involves the willingness and ability of the United States to help non-Communist states apply more acceptable popular programs for dealing with Asiatic nationalism and the fundamental urge to a higher standard of living. We must compete every inch of the way with the Soviet Union and the economic blueprint communism presents.

The real revolution in China is just starting, politically, economically and culturally, and the Chinese Communists are still a long way from success. But they already have attained power by concentrating on basic issues. Their prime slogans have been "anti-feudalism" and "anti-imperialism," both of which are designed to create far-reaching changes in China's economic structure, in its social relationships and in its international political orientation.

Unlike previous dynastic rulers, who achieved the Dragon Throne without making any fundamental changes in the Chinese way of life, the Communists have coupled their ascent to power with a well-defined program for drastic alterations in the pattern of existing society. That program—and the facts of geography, history and contemporary politics—point to the emergence in China of a new continental power. It will be a power which concentrates primarily on industrial rather than commercial development, which depends chiefly on the Soviet bloc for the creation of pilot industrial bases, and which coordinates its international policy with that of the Soviet Union.

This does not mean that the Communists will ignore—at least in certain areas—the possibilities of trade with the West on an unemotional, businesslike basis. From all indications, they are ready to trade with anyone able to deliver the goods they need and can afford, provided such deals do not undermine their political authority or threaten either their own or the Soviet Union's strategic interests. These conditions probably preclude trade with the West to any substantial degree in Manchuria, where the Soviet Union has carved out a tight sphere of economic as well as political influence.

If the Communists have any ruling passion within the context of their political ideology, it is a passion for industrialization through planning and control. All proclamations issued by Communist troops entering former Nationalist cities have warned the people not to destroy productive equipment on penalty of severe punishment. When a group of Communists in Southern Chahar permitted villagers to strip the Pang Chia-pu mine, a potentially important source of iron, the event was advertised widely by the controlled press as a "national scandal."

In emphasizing the need for increasing production and doing away with slovenly work habits, the Communist press features such "factory anecdotes" as the one entitled, "Li Ta Lan (Big Lazybones Li) Is Diligent Now." It tells of a shiftless factory hand who, when called to account by his fellows for lacking patriotism, finally replies: "You men will see. From now on I'll never drink and never gamble again. I'll be a new man from head to foot."

As part of the drive to make ends meet and boost the margin for productive expansion, the Communists are preaching a low-wage policy and austerity: be punctual, spend no longer than twenty minutes in the washroom, conserve electrical power, avoid waste, cut down on ceremonial gifts, avoid unnecessary feasts, eat "nourishing and cheap" foods, buy new clothing only when it is absolutely essential, and so on. In the midst of considerable unemployment created in Shanghai by takeover dislocations, the Kuomintang blockade and the disappearance of ECA aid, the Communists have told the people that—if necessary—"five persons should eat the rice of three."

Mao Tze-tung's "New Democracy" holds that China is not yet ready to enter the Socialist industrial era and that it must first go through an interim period in which relatively free play is given to capitalist forces.

Therefore the Communists have entered into an economic collaboration with the urban proletariat, the small land-owning peasant tillers, the private shopkeepers and the "national capitalists." The Chinese People's Republic established in Peiping is a coalition designed to reflect this economic entente in the political sphere. While the coalition includes non-Communist parties, however, it is completely dominated by the Reds.

According to the Communists this transitional period of state capitalism will be a fairly lengthy one. But it does not preclude, even in the era of the "New Democracy," the establishment of the kind of political controls that have become standard in all Communist-controlled countries.

All the instruments now at the command of the Communists—state power, the press, the radio, schools and thousands of party cadres enlisted from the ranks of enthusiastic students—already have been mobilized to break down old social values, create a politically loyal citizenry and establish a new cultural pattern more in keeping with the demands of the "New Democracy."

The Chinese press has been screened, combed out, re-licensed and uniformly regimented. Foreign missionaries are still being permitted to operate, but under new restrictions. The teaching of English is being de-emphasized and virtually all Western films have been banned.

Shanghai's bookshops have stocked new volumes on the works of Ma Ke-sze (Marx), Lieh Ning (Lenin), Sze Ta-lin (Stalin) and Mao Tze-tung. The school curricula have been revised. University students are now preoccupied with such courses as the "New Democracy," "Dialectical Materialism and the Materialist Concept of History," and "Recent Currents in Chinese Thought." And when he turns to his new primer on *kuo yu* (national language), the little second-grade shaver encounters as Lesson No. 1:

"It is red in the East. The sun is rising. Mao Tze-tung was born in China. He leads us to fight the enemy. We can be masters when the enemy is beaten. It is red in the East. The sun is rising. Mao Tze-tung was born in China. He leads us to make production. We will have food to eat, clothes to wear and not have to worry about poverty when the amount of production is increased."

In their attacks on Confucianism as "unscientific" and on the family system as a bar to higher social development, the Communists now demand for the state the Chinese citizen's primary loyalty. The constituent units of the family have been channeled into such organizations as trade unions, Poor Peasants' Associations, the Youth Corps, Children's Associations, Women's Associations and Housewives' Unions. Women have won a new freedom and, while the village oldsters moan about the breakup of the old society, the Housewives' Unions continue to sit in judgment on marital disputes and bring husbands to book for beating or otherwise oppressing their wives.

Thus, although the Chinese People's Republic is tightly controlled from the top, the average citizen is playing a far greater role in government than he has ever played before. Meetings and demonstrations proliferate. Every stratum of society has been tapped through the pervasive "study groups," a new and effective technique for mass re-education. The "study groups" extend into schools, factories, labor unions, guilds, government offices, clubs and almost every other kind of social cell.

In these ways, the Chinese Communist party has tackled the job of lifting 450,000,000 people up by their own bootstraps. Essentially, it is the same job with which the Nationalists were confronted when the war against Japan ended and on which they did not even get started, because of the civil war and glaring weaknesses that were inherent in the Nationalist regime itself.

Can the Communists succeed where the Nationalists failed? If by success is meant the ability of the Communists to turn China into a first-class industrial power and to raise the national standard of living dramatically within the next five or ten years, the answer is "No." On the other hand, if success is measured by their ability to maintain themselves in power, to overcome such opposition as may arise and to plug away at the job of reorganizing the country, the facts now available indicate that the answer is "Yes."

It is too early to assess the popularity—or unpopularity—of the Chinese revolution definitively, but certain facts can be recorded. Taking the lead in setting a model for strict honesty, zealousness and frugality, the Communists are getting considerable voluntary cooperation from students and professors, who now find greater leeway for their talents; from technicians, who now feel that they can really go to work on their machines; from politically conscious workers, who have won a new voice as leaders in the factory; and from a host of others who are tired of war and who are ready, for one reason or another, to come to terms with any regime that can hold power.

There is, on the other hand, much grumbling among shopkeepers who are being required to change their stock-in-trade (from jewelry, embroidered blouses and curios to shoes, hats and pots and pans), among workers who have been hard hit by the dislocation and the disruption of the export-import trade, and by coolies, office employes, chauffeurs and household servants who have been displaced by the departure of thousands of foreigners.

Another important and uncertain group is the Chinese peasant, who makes up 80 per cent of the population, who provided the Communists with the troops for seizing power, and who must create much of the margin for industrial development. The Communists won over the peasants by giving them land under a process of redistribution that may have made Chinese agriculture less, rather than more, efficient.

Recently, sporadic peasant uprisings have broken out in a number of places where the Communists have found it necessary to carry out food requisitions.

As a result the Communists are now talking about making farm plots larger rather than smaller. The peasant has thus become a potential enemy rather than an actual friend. The question of how desperate an enemy he becomes seems to depend on how far and how fast he is pushed.

But these uprisings have been quickly suppressed. And so far as potential resistance in the foreseeable future is concerned, it should not be forgotten that the Communists have at their disposal a loyal, well-indoctrinated, well-disciplined army of 4,000,000, that they are expanding the police functions of the state, and that the new central authority is on the verge of consolidating its power through zealous commissars over the whole China mainland.

The Chinese Communists required twenty-eight years to attain their present position. It is doubtful that they will give any opposition group the same political opportunities they exploited in attaining power.

Of course there is always the possibility of future changes within the party. Much depends on such factors as the efficacy of official policies, internal political rivalries, the demands Russia makes on the new regime, the ability of the Soviet Union to deliver the goods, and on how fast the Reds force the industrialization process.

The operational freedom of the Peiping regime in the economic sphere has been restricted by the Manchurian barter agreement, which prevents the Central Government from using Manchurian food surpluses to trade for industrial equipment on the world market. The development of Manchuria now depends on Soviet ability and willingness to industrialize an area that lies so close to American bases in Japan.

Although the real revolution in China, then, is far from over— is, in fact, just beginning, one thing remains clear. Notwithstanding the debates on who was responsible for what happened in China, the Communists are in control there. Their rise to power means a blackout for the flickering American picture of a China working painfully, but surely, toward the kind of society that would be politically and economically complementary to that of the United States.

Lacking an anti-Communist ally in China capable of winning the support of the Chinese people, we have lost the power to influence events there directly. With the British, the Indians, the French and even the Japanese anxious to resume normal political and trade relations with Communist China, we also have lost much of the power to influence events there indirectly.

The economic problems of the Chinese Communists may, in time, cause them to depend less exclusively than they do at present on the Soviet Union. But, for the time being at least—as Mao's trip to Moscow and his comments there have shown—that is a slim prospect and lies in the realm of wishful thinking.

It is by no means a simple matter. It involves area trade, raw materials for the industry of Japan, an acute shortage of administrators and technicians, the budgets and currencies of Britain, France and the Netherlands—and, for that matter, the budget of the United States.

Short of a return to pre-war Japanese fascism, the present choice in the Far East is between the kind of mixed parliamentary socialism established in India—capable of defending itself against Japanese efforts to overthrow it—and the kind of mixed Communist-sponsored socialism established in China. Extending the Indian type of regime throughout East Asia, with its weak indigenous political and administrative systems outside India, promises to be far more difficult than extending the Chinese type of police-socialism. Nevertheless, this is the challenge we must face. And in the long run, the pay-off is going to be not in terms of which side has the best platitudes, but of which side has the best program and the most effective approach.

Report on Okinawa:
A Rampart We Built

by George Barrett

OKINAWA.

ON WAR MAPS in Peiping's moated Imperial Palace and Moscow's white-arched Building of the Red Army some special warning symbols certainly have been crayoned around Okinawa, this spot of Pacific coral where the last battle of World War II was fought—and from which the Western powers may well make their first major counterstrike if the Communists set off world war III.

This barrier-reefed outpost was little more than a wasteland when the last war ended here seven years ago. But what was still only recently a lonely, weed-ravaged memorial to the 12,520 Americans and 110,000 Japanese who died in the savage transfer of title has become a rivet-hammering, rock-blasting, $500,-000,000 construction project.

The island, only 400 miles from the Communist-conquered mainland of China, has gone through one of the amazing transformations in the history of Pacific defenses. A 500-square-mile patch of once desolate subtropics, smaller than the Shetlands and

From the *New York Times Magazine*, September 21, 1952, copyright © 1952 by The New York Times Company.

less than half the size of Rhode Island, it has quietly mushroomed into a first-class island bastion, barbed with batteries of long-muzzled 120's cannonading in watchful practice across the emerald waters of the China Sea. Whole complexes of airports pack the sun-baked flatlands, forming a sprawling airdrome for the B-29's that take off each day to pound North Korea; for the hissing Starfires and Shooting Stars on constant prowl against sudden enemy attacks; and—if war comes—for the gargantuan eight-engine heavies that can carry atom bombs against any target on the surface of our planet.

Okinawa, living down its G. I. reputation as an "outpost for the outcast," is now a collection—almost a magical transplanting—of whole American communities, with several more still building. Some of these are already complete, even to schools, department stores, theatres and suburban housing developments boasting winding roads, flagstone walks and "picket" fences made of bamboo.

The war that was so short a time ago, and the war that is here again, and the next war which, if it comes, would engulf Okinawa for a third time, have created a weird pattern of contrasts, an amalgam in mood of war and peace, an amalgam in time of past, present and future, and even a weird amalgam of sounds: kids yelling "Heigh-ho, Silver!" around backyard clotheslines; four-engined bombers thrumming in unnoticed take-offs, Korea-bound; an almost symphonic tone poem of construction notes from Diesel-powered Letourneau carriers and steam-hammered pile drivers, and a competitive counterpoint provided by a throaty, primeval chorus of snake-tailed geckos, glass-winged dragonflies and black-bell crickets.

Working against typhoons, against the long supply haul across the vast Pacific, against the operating demands of daily bomb strikes on enemy installations, and against time itself—while the world wonders where the next Communist attack will hit—construction gangs of Americans, Okinawans, Filipinos and Japanese have converted this central island of the Ryukyuan chain into the key American air base in the Far East.

Okinawa assures, if not command of the airways in this part of the world, at least impressive range for Allied air strikes against the industrial hearts of the two great Communist powers, China and Russia. It is pointed out by Maj. Gen. Robert S. Beightler, commander of the island fortress, that present-day bombers, flying from these coral shores, can dominate every potential target in the vast land mass of Asia.

Specifically, even today's bombers—"babies" compared to the jet monsters for which runways are now being built here—can reach over into any area of the Far East that is vital to the Communists or threatened by them—the whole of Southeast Asia, all of modern China, all of Russia's Lake Baikal industrial region, the whole of eastern Siberia and the southern tip of the Kamchatka peninsula, the potential Red springboard for any attack on the Aleutian outposts of the American mainland.

There is a lot about Okinawa, present and potential, that falls under the classification of secret, and, as one official here explained wryly, some things here are so secret that even the names given to their classification of secrecy are secret. Generally speaking, Okinawa is for the Air Force what Pearl Harbor is for the Navy, but perhaps a better gauge of its all-round military importance is the title this island has been informally given—the Triple-A Threat.

That means attack—attack by air, attack by airborne, attack by amphibious. General Beightler, who led the Thirty-seventh Infantry Division through more than three and one-half years of Pacific fighting in the second World War, has set out to construct, not only one of the world's greatest bomber bases, but also a potential staging area from which either amphibious or airborne operations could be launched.

While Okinawa is probably too small to be used as a jump-off point for any mass operation against, for example, Chinese armies on the mainland, its relation to possible future wars, aside from the air aspects, is perhaps best defined by the past, when the whole Allied campaign against Japan was predicated on the seizure and use of Okinawa as a main springboard.

Then, a total of 182,821 Allied troops were stationed in the Ryukyus, the vast majority of them here on Okinawa, and all of them supplied over the beaches and through almost totally destroyed ports. Now, as the official accounting puts it, "with the improvements that have been made in the port facilities, road nets, communication facilities, utilities, storage facilities and airfields, the total number of troops which could be staged through Okinawa should far exceed the number stationed there during the last war."

Essentially, however, these are correlative uses as far as Okinawa is concerned. It is as a bomber bastion, a "Gibraltar of the Pacific," that the new Okinawa is designed—both a base of origin and a stop-over in hemispheric bomb strikes.

Okinawa's special importance derives from the fact that it should be possible to keep this island as a forward base when other airfields outside the continental limits of the United States are lost to us, either for military or political reasons.

This centrally sited island, flanked on both sides by protective island outposts, is easily defended against enemy invasion. In its native meaning, the name given to the Ryukyus is "Floating Rope," a title that neatly spells out the fluid use of them either as a defensive barrier or as a strangulating weapon. (Some of the other names given by the Japanese many years ago to Okinawa sites, and retained by American military authorities, still have perfect meanings; Futema Airfield, for example, is best translated as the "Airfield of the War God.")

Radar nets keep unblinking eyes on all movements on the long stretches of the East China Sea and the Philippine Sea surrounding Okinawa, and where sampan invasion fleets out of China's coast might well be able to make landings on neighboring places like Formosa, enemy ships and planes have too much water to cross to be able to reach Okinawa without telegraphing their course far in advance.

Mobile batteries of guns also keep sentry on the shores day and night. (Things here are on a big scale, and one target practice session for one battery of four guns costs $60,000 in shells.) General Beightler has mobilized even the cooks and clerks and special services personnel into combat companies to be ready to drop their skillets and their pens and join in the defense of the island bastion.

As far as anybody can determine, there is little or no danger of native fifth column activity, one of the crucial considerations most military commanders must face these days wherever war breaks out with the Communists, particularly in the Far East. There are about 580,000 natives on Okinawa; their ties, culturally, psychologically and historically, are firmly with Japan, and it is the rare Okinawan who will not volunteer the hope that Okinawa will someday be turned back to Japanese sovereignty.

But this in no sense implies anti-Americanism. The swift pace of the conversion process into a major air base leaves many of the leisure-loving Okinawans somewhat confused, and when you get among some of the Okinawans who like to remember how the Japanese treated them as country cousins, usually kindly, you discover some resentment over Army signs that say "Off Limits" and "No Okinawans Allowed." Most Okinawans, however, are today, even with their communities still far from rebuilt after the war, better off economically than they were under the Japanese.

The average Okinawan says he wants his island to go back to Japan because that is the "fatherland." But until that occurs, as nearly as can be figured out by most political observers, what most Okinawans would like is for the American military establishment to remain, to keep building, to improve the local economy as it has for several years.

The political future of the islands is still deep in the shadows, but at the moment it seems highly unlikely that the United States is pouring so many millions into a strategic air base just to turn it back, when it is precisely the fact that Okinawa is now under our complete control that helps to make the island as militarily attractive as it is. However, great pains are being taken, under a special Government section of the command, to tutor the Okinawans and other Ryukyuans in the ways of democratic administration. Under the Army the Ryukyuans have had island-wide free elections, something they never enjoyed under the Japanese.

For many of them the arrival of Americans has meant a transformation in living patterns that they relish: native women in smart Sears, Roebuck frocks and permanent waves (many of them still carry babies sling-fashion on their backs and beat the family wash on river rocks); young Okinawans, both boys and girls, proudly chauffeuring big sedans and driving massive six-wheeled Euclid dump trucks; humor-fond Ryukyuans grinning at the safety posters of the Red Man caricature from Dogpatch, grunting: "Accidents Is 100 per cent (Ugh) Un-American."

Then there are those who work for the Army, like 23-year-old Miyoko Nagimine, who, seven years ago, went with several hundred high school students to the Kenji caves in a pact to commit mass suicide rather than fall into the hands of the United States Army. When her schoolmates clasped hands and jumped into the sea, Miyoko thought it over again and decided to wait. Today she works contentedly for the United States Army.

The construction project, which in effect is converting the lower third of Okinawa from tropical barrenness into a series of self-contained communities, is roughly equivalent in manpower effort, according to engineers here, to building a city the size of Indianapolis from scratch. Back in 1946 there were amazed reactions to the scope of construction at Oak Ridge; today Oak Ridge would fit easily into any one of the four major building compounds under construction on Okinawa.

Some 4,000 cement-block houses, most of them with double patios, three bedrooms and completely modern kitchens, are going up for use by officers and their families and top-grade G. I.'s with their families. Also under way are sixty-five casement-windowed, company-sized barracks, where soldiers and airmen still tell each other they never had it so good, only here they usually mean it. Chintz curtains on the windows, four-man tables in company dining rooms adorned by tropical blossoms and clean linens, full-length mirrors in white-tiled washrooms, and houseboys and maids who lose face if a G. I. tries to sew on his own buttons, are some of the "built-in" features.

Nobody wants to talk here in terms of precise construction statistics that might give away some of the military developments, but they will break down the over-all picture enough to disclose that the several communities with their schools and stores and club houses and block after block of residential homes account for only 25 per cent of the Okinawan project—all the rest is military.

Here are some thumb-nail images:

If all the asphaltic concrete used on Okinawa could be put into a single-lane road 11 feet wide the highway would go from New York to Chicago; if the poured concrete could be formed into a sidewalk 4 feet wide it would start at New York and end in San Francisco; and if the cement blocks could be laid end to end in the United States they would make a wall 4 feet high completely across the country, with an extension of another 1,000 miles into the sea.

This mammoth construction job has been carried on against nature's full arsenal of resistance. Heat in summer at 90 or more, humidity usually around 90 per cent. San Francisco is supposed to be a soggy city, with 20 inches of rainfall each year, but Okinawa averages 80 to 85 inches annually. It's the typhoons, however, that have raised real havoc. As many as forty-five typhoons may touch Okinawa in a single year and three to six of these pass directly over the island.

Not so long ago one typhoon hit so hard that in military losses alone the damage exceeded $100,000,000. But through trial and error, and after many nasty bruises, a system has now been worked out that strips most of the ferocity from the 150-mile-an-hour winds.

A warning system very similar to air-raid alerts is maintained, with typhoon wardens stationed at key spots of the island, and as the "enemy" approaches preparations here shift rapidly from the simple warning of Condition Three to the Urgent Batten Down warning of Condition One. By the time the typhoon's shrieking vanguard blasts race in across the wave-whipped shores every man is snug in a typhoon shelter, the buildings are cabled solidly to the ground and the larders are comfortably packed with rations to last two to four days.

Typhoons, in fact, have become something of a bore. This correspondent sat out Typhoon Karen a couple of weeks ago, and came up with these skits of unexcitability: the stenographer, GS rating 5, petulantly folding up her typewriter and muttering, "Damn, I wanted to see the Will Rogers movie tonight"; the kids and the Air Force pilots lining up at the PX to buy a reserve store of comic books; the canasta couples pooling their canned goods for dinners and lunches and breakfasts of cold beans, preserved fruits and sandwiches while the storm rages—but first feasting on a quick banquet of steak plus chicken plus roast beef before the refrigerator goes out and the meat spoils; the colonel cradling three bottles of gin in his arms and happily announcing. "Let 'er blow!"

There are tableaux in Okinawa that are not so casual. The wife and the 7-year-old in his mail-order spurs seeing daddy off in his silvered B-29, and the very slow wave of mama's hand in unspoken good-by.

And her neighbor two rows across, five houses down—she's not waiting any more. It has been eleven weeks since her husband flew to, but not from, North Korea. The Air Force intelligence major said not to "blow apart," that sometimes pilots are able to parachute out and officially her husband is only MIA—Missing in Action. But she has been listening to the Pyongyang broadcasts and his name has never been mentioned, and the Air Force may soon be stopping the pay and allowances, and she thinks she should pack up and get Jimmy, Billy and Cissie home—somewhere—before that happens.

Such reminders of the war now being fought from these shores seem sometimes out of place in an atmosphere that most G. I.'s call "solid Stateside." Despite the intensity and range of planning and construction, duty for the 40,000 civilian and military personnel is pretty much a 40-hour-a-week proposition. Stores and shops and post offices close over the week-ends, and it's asking for domestic trouble if you forget to reserve Wednesday night for bingo with your wife or your date.

The Cup and Saucer, a soda-fountain hangout for the 'teenage set (complete with bobby socks and blue jeans) and for the hit-and-run coffee crowd, does a rush-order business in "tin roof sundaes," and any car customer who wants to spend an extra five cents for the take-out service can get it from jaunty-capped soda clerks—Okinawan—who look as though they have just stepped out of a Howard Johnson's.

Off duty, the troops can wear civvies, which here take on the dazzling form of Aloha shirts for the G. I.'s and bare-shoulder cotton frocks for the Wacs.

There are many old-time Army residents here—by choice—men like Master Sgt. John S. Cupples of Gary, Ind., who is now in his fourth voluntary extension on the island. A long time ago he had a leave in Japan, but he broke it off; he says he wanted "to come home."

Sgt. John W. Larabee, from Kansas City, Mo., who is living with his wife Janet in a cozy five-room house, says that when he came here three years ago Okinawa was famous for its desolation —its "rust, rot and ruin"—but life has become so pleasant on the coral spit that he and his wife would like to extend their stay if only the Army would let them.

There are some real surprises on Okinawa, including what Okinawans themselves think about it. Maj. Maurice R. Fowler and his wife Bernice took a Sunday drive a few weeks ago to the "untouched" section to the north and excitedly brought out their camera when they suddenly spotted a picturesque native farmer, barefoot, with a conical straw hat on his head and a primitive shoulder-haul for carrying two huge baskets of sweet potatoes.

His name was Es Nakada, he spoke smooth English, and he had moved back to Okinawa from California. "Too hot there," he said.

The full measure of what life has come to mean here for Americans assigned to Okinawa is given in the story of the captain and the major. For four years Capt. Lowell K. Schmid, who calls

New Rochelle his home, was separated by Army assignment from his wife, Waf Maj. Umbria J. Schmid, who was serving most of that time in Germany while he was posted at Fort Slocum. Three months ago the captain and the major were transferred by joint orders to Okinawa. But until the next batch of new houses is completed the captain must continue to live in bachelor officers' quarters and the major must continue to live in the Waf billets.

And the captain and the major say that they like Okinawa.

The Touchy Issue
of Peace with Japan

by Lindesay Parrott

TOKYO.

IN ANCIENT Japanese animal chronology 1950 is "the year of the tiger," which comes once every twelve years and is a lucky year. It is even "the year of the five yellow tigers," which under the same system repeats itself once in thirty-seven years and is still luckier. Until the signing of the thirty-year agreement between Communist China and Soviet Russia, the Japanese were convinced that this was also to be "the year of the peace treaty," which again will restore to Japan her national sovereignty with sins and penalties of the war expunged and all-important "face" restored.

Whether they believe in tigers, the Japanese still have reasons for believing in a peace treaty. The United States has been framing a new policy for Asia after the Communist victories in China. This has been put in charge of Ambassador Philip Jessup—and the Japanese were impressed by the Ambassador's visit to Tokyo —indicating Japan's new problems will be taken up under the new program.

From the *New York Times Magazine,* February 26, 1950, copyright © 1950 by The New York Times Company.

Another significant development was the trip to Japan of the United States Chiefs of Staff, which the Japanese associated with General MacArthur's statement that Japan has merited a peace treaty by its conduct under the occupation.

Certainly complicating factors recently have been introduced with British recognition of the Chinese Communist regime, from which the United States withholds approval, and with the Sino-Soviet agreement. It is difficult to see how the Commonwealth nations could act on the treaty without participation of the Chinese Government they recognize. Nor is it apparent how the United States, not recognizing the Communists, could include them in the negotiations. Most important, the Sino-Soviet pact, which stated that China and Russia seek a quick peace with Japan, is regarded here as a direct warning against a separate Japanese peace with the West.

On this basis some commentators in the Japanese press recently have been indicating a belief that the treaty again must indefinitely be delayed—though this plainly is not the view of the Japanese Government. Nevertheless, the Japanese can argue that the fall of China to the Communists actually has advanced rather than retarded the cause of a "separate" treaty with the Western nations, which they have been led to expect.

The situation has changed vastly since the treaty first began to be discussed in 1947. In those days the "cold war" in Asia was still in a rather academic stage and it was possible to talk of the future of Japan without undue pressure from events. This is no longer true. Not only is China gone but Formosa may fall into the hands of the Communists. Should the Communists incorporate Formosa in their system the importance of Japan as an advanced democratic foothold in the Pacific would be magnified.

The possibility that Japan itself might be taken over by the Communists must be considered. While the occupation continues, there is small likelihood of this happening, but what can be said about the future—if American troops are withdrawn? It must be remembered that, if after rehabilitating Japan, we allow the country to slip into Communist hands, we have handed them on a silver platter precisely what Russia has been seeking and failing to obtain since the Russo-Japanese War more than forty years ago—an industrial plant in the Far East.

It is scarcely likely that the Soviet demand for the trial of the Emperor as a war criminal will ever develop into a factor affecting the peace settlement. No one, including the Russians, believed that the demand would be granted, and here it was generally regarded as illegal under post-war international practice. The Soviet, as Washington pointed out, agreed originally with the Far Eastern Commission, of which it is a member, that the Emperor should be excluded from the war criminal trial list. Now, four and one-half years after Japan's surrender and a year after the war trial court's dissolution, Russia's assertion of Hirohito's criminality, without offering even a shadow of new evidence, was a step which was hard to take seriously.

Officially the view taken here is that the Russians introduced their demand more to distract attention from their failure to repatriate more than 30,000 Japanese war prisoners than with any idea of affecting the treaty talks. But as far as the treaty is concerned, the Soviet demand did underline that Russia would refuse negotiations with the Japanese Government headed even nominally by a man she considers a war criminal. This attitude has long been evident, and the only question really at issue is whether there could be a peace treaty signed by some, probably a majority of the eleven nations of the Far Eastern Commission, without the others.

What, then, are the advantages to the United States of signing the peace treaty now, and what are the obstacles? The advantages, it might be answered, are primarily moral ones and the difficulties are those of the physical complications. The advantages lie in the opportunity to demonstrate:

(1) That the United States meant what it said in the Potsdam agreement—that independence be granted to Japan and formal occupation removed after certain conditions were fulfilled—and, despite the changed international situation, has no intention of going back on its word.

(2) That the Western democracies are willing to assure at least

comparative self-rule and guarantee comparative prosperity to nations genuinely willing to follow the democratic path.

(3) That there is no truth, as far as Japan is concerned, in the repeated Communist assertion that the United States is out to "colonialize" in Asia and that, instead, it is removing a large measure of control.

(4) That the United States is willing to trust Japan to become a bulwark of democracy in the Pacific and does not feel it necessary to maintain complete management of all Japanese affairs in order to see that this becomes the case.

Such a policy could become of considerable importance in Asia. It would presumably encourage what democratic elements exist. It probably would present an increasing contrast between the fate of nations which pin their faith on the democracies and those which join or are taken over by Communist régimes.

The Orient and the world already understand what has happened to the Soviet Union's eastern European satellites. It is more than probable that they will see the same thing again in Communist China. The contrast might become of enormous value to the Western cause in oriental countries still hesitating between two allegiances.

The difficulties for the United States in connection with a treaty, unfortunately more apparent than the potential advantages, can be summarized as follows:

(1) Most important is that the action would force a new open break between the West and its former Pacific allies. Since there is no agreement between the United States and the Soviet Union either on the terms of a treaty or even on the manner in which a draft shall be framed, unilateral action by the West again would emphasize the wide differences between the two camps and possibly suggest to the Asiatic nations that they can hold a bargaining position in the middle. This some Japanese already have found an interesting subject for speculation and would be willing to try out.

(2) Another element is that the United States after the treaty would have to allay fears in the Far East—Australia and the Phil-

ippines may serve as examples—that America is willing again to build a strong, potentially aggressive Japan as a weapon in the ideological war against Russia without reference to a possible backfire should Japan again become powerful enough to dominate the Western Pacific either by itself or by changing sides for a price.

(3) There is a question whether an independent Japan in the long run might prove an ally or enemy in the Pacific. Plainly Japan must be restored to independence if United States pledges are to be carried out and propaganda value extracted from them. Plainly, too, it is a risk for the United States to finance and rehabilitate Japan as we financed and armed China, only to find the effort, in effect, had advanced the Communist cause. It would be a tragic mistake.

These are practical considerations which must be weighed, and it may be that conditions of the post-war world make them more important than moral issues.

The Potsdam Declaration serves as a yardstick to measure Japan's positive accomplishments. Here are some of the actions taken to carry out vital clauses of the declaration:

(1) Dictator Tojo, most of his Cabinet and many of his military leaders have been tried and sentenced. Japan may become a military nation once more but it will never again be led by this group.

(2) Last October General Headquarters announced that the war crimes trials in Japan had come to an end after about 1,000 prisoners had been brought before United States Military Commissions here. There was a total of about 4,200 convictions throughout the Far East.

(3) Freedom of speech, religion and thought, as well as respect for fundamental rights, have been established, say the Japanese—and General MacArthur has agreed with them—by the new Constitution, with its Bill of Rights. The series of elections held under the new Constitution, which have given the Japanese administrations ranging from socialist to conservative, would indicate that "there has been established, in accordance with the freely

expressed will of the Japanese people, a peacefully inclined and responsible Government," as Potsdam prescribed.

Thus, technically at least, it can be argued that the terms of Potsdam have been complied with and the Japanese have a right to ask that the West now carry out its end of the bargain by withdrawing the occupation forces.

But how far has Japan been converted to democracy? It would be a bold analyst who would attempt to give a positive answer. On paper the Occupation has given the Japanese all the most modern democratic trimmings from the free ballot box to votes for women, to free school lunches and a land-reform program.

How much of this system have the Japanese wanted and how much was merely accepted as the will of the victors? Probably most Japanese approved some of it and some Japanese most of it. But it must not be forgotten that Japan is an old country with a long tradition of which democracy is not a natural part. It has been a nation of caste and power concentrations which has often preferred strong leadership to thinking for itself. Even its willingness to accept the Occupation's orders to change may serve as an example.

Some Japanese groups are in active opposition to democracy as America understands it. The so-called "danger from the Right" in the official points of view is largely illusory, though there are little groups of ex-soldiers which might conceivably prove dangerous in certain circumstances. But the Japanese Communist party scarcely can be disregarded.

Few here in this correspondent's observation agree wholeheartedly with General MacArthur's September declaration: "The threat of communism as a major issue in Japanese life is past. It fell by its own excesses." It is true, and this is probably what the General meant, that the Communist movement in the past year has reached about its lowest ebb since the surrender. Its grip on the labor unions is plainly breaking and opinion polls and by-elections indicate that it is losing popular support.

Meanwhile, the Japanese Communist party is still estimated to have 190,000 members and possibly a couple of million supporters. It is financially well-heeled. It has got definite plans for violent revolution, according to recent findings of the Diet investigating committee, and it is cocky with the example of Communist victories in China.

What most Japanese believe is that the Communists are lying low awaiting the departure of the Occupation to make a big drive to take over. It is plainly one sizable group of Japanese which has not been converted to democracy.

Japan's economic situation, too, presents a two-sided picture. The gains were pointed out by General MacArthur and some figures given—coal production up, exports increasing, trade now established with more than a score of countries. It was the General's statement that Japan now is "rapidly" moving toward the 1930-34 level which tentatively was set for her post-war economy by the Far Eastern Commission.

A walk through any Tokyo department store is convincing, too. The capital is far from the days when the only goods available were such simple instruments as could be hammered out of the discarded helmets of demobilized soldiers. It has been remarked, "You can buy anything in Tokyo today," and it is probably true that actual production considerably exceeds that which shows on the books.

It must be remembered that the Japanese economic revival, like Japanese democratic progress, has been accomplished under tight Occupation control, and that the United States since the end of the war has been providing about half a billion dollars a year to meet deficits which Japanese economy has been unable to supply—largely food.

Meanwhile, fundamental Japanese problems—the same problems which, many Japanese argue, forced this nation to go to war in the Pacific—remain or are intensified. The population, already too large, has increased by leaps and bounds since the surrender—at the rate of more than a million annually. Japan's land area limits food production, and forces the nation to import or starve. Some overseas markets, like Manchuria and China, seem to have disappeared and in others there is a dwindling demand for Japanese goods of pre-war character—silk in the United States, for instance.

Certainly Japan, disarmed and stripped of much war potential, could not, even if willing and permitted to do so, carry on the smallest aggressive movement in Asia. But the Japanese, with some justification, still consider themselves the best—certainly industrially the ablest—people in Asia and it is scarcely likely that they would consent permanently to go hungry while supplies existed close at hand.

What might result, if Japan's economy got into trouble, would be violent revolution to overthrow a profitless democratic connection and a turn for salvation to a new totalitarianism of the Left and a reliance on the resources of the Communist countries of Asia which could use Japanese industrial power. This possibility the treaty makers must consider.

These are what might be termed the internal considerations, but equally important, and far more discussed here, are the external considerations—the problem of Japan's foreign relations when she again becomes technically an independent nation. Perhaps Japan's primary problem, therefore, will be one of defense.

From the outset it is realized here that Japan's situation will be extremely tricky. For should the United States and Britain sign treaties with Japan, and the Soviet Union and Communist China abstain, then Japan would be at peace with some of her former enemies but still technically at war with others. How, in these circumstances, would Japan be guaranteed against possible foreign aggression?

Japan, in the opinion of this correspondent, has no desire to fight again. She has no desire to be forced into either an Eastern or Western bloc in a third world war which again might make her an atomic battlefield. It is true, undoubtedly, as Lieut. Gen. Robert L. Eichelberger, former commander of the United States Eighth Army here, has repeatedly pointed out, that Japan would make a valuable ally should a "hot war" come between the United States and Russia. The combat abilities of the Japanese soldier are well known to him.

But Japan, I think, would make a reluctant ally without much will to fight on either side even if armed and equipped from outside, as she presumably would have to be. The question is, how could Japan stay out of a new world war?

Short of a "third force" which Japan might join in holding the balance between the world's two conflicting ideologies—something that has not yet appeared—it is almost impossible to see how Japan after a treaty could long avoid standing up and being counted on one side or the other.

The alternative to this is the defensive rearmament of Japan after the repeal of the constitutional article against maintenance of an armed force. Technically, in the opinion of experts, this probably could be done. Such things as light automatic weapons, short-range interceptor planes, coast defense equipment, which Japan now lacks, scarcely could be considered means of aggression. It has been argued in some circles that Japan should be allowed these and then should undertake the burden of her own defense.

But here also many problems arise. The first is whether any of Japan's former enemies could see their way clear to permitting even such weapons to Japan—and some certainly would raise the most violent objections. Hitler's rearmament of Germany from the small cadres the Allies originally permitted is a historic object lesson which comes to mind.

Even should permission be granted, Japan, bankrupt since the Pacific war, could not afford even the smallest military expenditure in a national budget already deep in deficits. On the other hand, should weapons be provided, Japan automatically would be enlisted on the side of whatever bloc supplied them—or at least would be so regarded by opponents. Neutrality would then again be gone.

Another proposal is retention of a foreign protective force even after the treaty is signed, and this, it is believed here, probably will be the answer. The Occupation would technically be withdrawn. What would remain might be called a constabulary, an international police, or by any other name. In fact, it would have the same military function as the Occupation fulfills today—without its administrative duties.

To such forces bases might be leased, as, for instance, the United States leases bases in the independent Philippines, and this might be provided for either in the treaty itself or in a parallel agreement between Japan and the protecting power or powers.

The United States after four years cannot now wash its hands of Japan unless it is prepared to see the disintegration of almost everything built here since the surrender. Japanese democracy, such as it is, exists by virtue of the United States and must continue to do so for some time to come. In the opinion of this observer, who has been here since the beginning, there are three major considerations the treaty must deal with in one way or another if the system that we have founded here is to be maintained.

First, it would be dangerous if not suicidal to try the new Japanese democracy too severely. It is arguable at least that the United States contributed to the downfall of China when after the war it thrust upon the Chinese National Government responsibilities of national reorganization which the Government proved unable to accomplish. If similar mistakes are not to be made here, it will be necessary to keep in Japan for some years some form of supervisory mechanism to assure that the Potsdam terms remain fulfilled.

It is objected that this would limit the new sovereignty of Japan. It must be pointed out that such a system presumably would have the support of those Japanese—and there are many—who fear the end of the Occupation. This point of view was emphasized recently by Japanese officials who deplored General MacArthur's removal of United States civil affairs teams from the prefectures.

Second, some form of protection must be given to Japan, both internal and external. Internally, as has been pointed out, Japan has a predatory, well-organized and violent minority in its Communists. This has been dealt with to date primarily by the Occupation, which has suppressed violence where necessary but has avoided making martyrs.

Responsibility for the continued internal order in Japan, it would seem, remains with us at least until it is proved that the Japanese Government has the power and determination to check outbreaks and the common sense to realize that there is nothing to be gained by the establishment of a right totalitarianism to fight a left totalitarianism.

Third, Japan is going to need economic assistance also for some time to come, probably at about the same rate as at present. This aid is now supplied by the GARIOA and EROA agencies. Both these funds and foreign-currency expenditures from Japanese Government holdings in the United States are under American supervision.

The United States through some agency—perhaps some form of Asiatic Marshall Plan—not only will have to continue to finance Japan for some years but will have the duty to its own taxpayers of seeing that the funds are expended to the best possible advantage, as it does at present.

These are some of the problems the treaty makers have to face. What they envisage, if the solutions suggested above are valid, are increased autonomy, but not complete independence for some years to come for a Japan which is more or less tightly tied into the Western democratic group.

Gigantic Questions for Mao —And for Us, Too

by Henry R. Lieberman

OF ALL THE gifts that went to Joseph Stalin on his seventieth birthday, Mao Tze-tung's was probably the most impressive. His pilgrimage to Moscow and his praise of Stalin as the "teacher and friend" of the Chinese people symbolized the developing alliance of the two largest Communist countries on earth. It also served to dispel—at least for the time being—the wishful hopes in the West that Mao Tze-tung might turn out to be an Asiatic Tito.

There was nothing startling about Mao's trip, for he has now been on record for some time as accepting the primacy of Stalin as the world's No. 1 Communist figure. Last July, for example, in his brochure, "On the People's Democratic Dictatorship," he emphasized that China would "lean to one side" and that there was no middle course. He added: "Internationally, we belong to the anti-imperialist front headed by the U.S.S.R., and we can only look for genuinely friendly aid from that front, and not from the imperialist front."

This reference to assistance from the Soviet front suggests that the importance, first of the atom bomb, and now of the hydrogen bomb, in this context is that it may cause the Bolsheviks to think again. It was all very fine and easy for Lenin to talk about communism rising like the phoenix from the ashes of war in the pre-atomic era. But we have now reached the stage where nobody remotely in his senses could imagine that reciprocal destruction, on a scale now freely envisaged, can prepare the way for the organized dictatorship of the proletariat or for anything but universal ruin. And if Stalin is forced to modify Bolshevik teaching on the place of war in the Leninist-Marxist system, he will be forced sooner or later to modify other important aspects of that teaching.

When we speak of war between Russia and the West we mean total war. In the eyes of its rulers, the Soviet Union has been at war with the non-Communist world for over thirty years—since Lenin made Russia the base for his own private war against that world, which at that time was the whole planet, except for 100,000 Bolsheviks. This state of war has existed ever since, though concealed at times in one way or another, for purely tactical reasons. After a brief offensive in the early days, Russia went over to the defensive with the slogan of "Socialism in One Country." The main objective was to turn the U.S.S.R. into an invulnerable base for world revolution.

The principles of this war were laid down in Lenin's innumerable writings. The main body of his teaching, in this sense, has been renashed by Stalin in "Problems of Leninism" and "A Short History of the Communist Party of the U.S.S.R.," both of which are compulsory reading for all Communists. As manifested today, the principles call for the strengthening of the Soviet Union as a defensive base for communism, the weakening by all possible means of non-Communist powers, the prevention of anti-Communist coalitions, and the fostering of revolutionary movements in other lands, in so far as these can be subordinated to the Communist party of the U.S.S.R.

Nothing could be more lucid in theory or more complicated in practice. The complications arise from the fact that there are frequent contradictions between the internal needs and the external policy of the Kremlin—i.e., the desire to exploit a revolutionary situation abroad may conflict with the need to build up strength and morale at home.

If the theory is lucid, the practice is tortuous and involved. The methods called for are in essence the tactics of the Trojan horse, ramified in every conceivable way and complicated by an instant readiness to sacrifice the whole apparatus to the enemy should such an action seem expedient. The general line is conveniently outlined by Lenin himself in his celebrated pamphlet, "Left Wing Communism: An Infantile Disorder," written shortly before his death and dedicated in an ironical spirit to David Lloyd George, then the British Prime Minister.

Lenin says: "It is possible to conquer a powerful enemy only by exerting the most intense effort, by taking thorough, attentive, meticulous and skillful advantage of each and every split among the bourgeois of the various countries, and by taking advantage of every opportunity, even the most trivial, to gain a mass ally, though this ally may be temporary and unstable, vacillating, conditional, and unreliable."

The most recent statement of Soviet war aims was made in a special Pravda article by Lavrenti Beria, one of the new triumvirate now ruling the Soviet Union under Stalin. The article was written for his master's seventieth birthday.

"Stalin has laid down a program of action for Communists. They must (1) exploit all differences and contradictions in the bourgeois camp; (2) take concrete action to unite the working classes of the economically advanced countries with the national liberation movement in the colonies and dependent nations; (3) complete the struggle for unity of the trade union movement; (4) take active measures to bring together the proletariat and the small peasants; (5) support Soviet rule and disrupt the interventionist machinations of imperialism against the Soviet Union, bearing in mind that the Soviet Union is the base of revolutionary movement in all countries."

Thus, in practice, the present aims of Soviet foreign policy, which is a belligerent policy, may be summarized as an effort to achieve without war certain objectives of a kind traditionally achieved by war: the ruin of Western economy; the integration of the satellites with the Soviet economy; the penetration of Asia; the overthrow of sovereign governments in non-Communist countries. A principal way of achieving this is to weaken opposition and divide it. Particular activities, like the Communist offensives in Italy and France, the Berlin blockade, the Partisans of Peace movement, the attack on colonial empires, attempts to intimidate Turkey and Iran, the betrayal of the Jews, the disrupting of the United Nations, all fit themselves into one or another of the main objectives.

But our real question is whether, in the next five years, or fifteen years, or ever, total war is likely to seem to Moscow a better means toward the ultimate objective than the sort of policies preached by both Lenin and Stalin and, until now, practiced with steadfastness and restraint.

To anyone who knows Russia and the Russians, the idea of Moscow starting, or deliberately and consciously risking total war —which means, in practice, a shooting war with America and the British Empire—within the next five years is so absurd that it is impossible to consider it seriously. The Soviet Union would be quite incapable of sustaining an aggressive war against the United States and the British Empire in the next five years because it is too weak materially and too divided internally—to say nothing of the fact that it is engaged in holding down by force, or the threat of force, a ring of satellites looking for war as the signal for revolt.

Materially, the U.S.S.R. has a population of close to 200,000,-000, at least a third as much again as the population of the United States. This vast population is scheduled this year to produce 250,-000,000 tons of coal as against America's 1949 production of 435,000,000, and 35,000,000 tons of steel as against America's 77,868,000, 35,000,000 tons of oil as against America's 315,000,-000. These moderate figures show a strong recovery from the post-war position and an increase on the 1940 level. They absorb the whole energies of government and people, the immense mass of the laboring classes working for a bare subsistence under conditions of extreme harshness and privation in order to fulfill the

Plans. In 1940 the figures were, coal, 164,000,000 tons; steel, 18,-000,000 tons and oil, 30,000,000 tons. With this level of production, and materially assisted by America and the British Empire, Russia only just managed to pull victoriously through the fight with Germany, at the cost of untold devastation, sporadic famine, universal undernourishment, the total dislocation of her whole economy and the active revolt of millions of her minority nationalities.

The farthest Russia now looks ahead is to 1960. Five years ago Stalin gave as the target for that year, "at the earliest," 60,000,000 tons of steel, 60,000,000 tons of oil and 500,000,000 tons of coal. "Only under such conditions," he said, "can we regard our country as guaranteed against any accidents. This will require perhaps three new Five-Year Plans if not more." All the signs show that it will require more.

The Russian people have been driven too hard for too long, in exchange for too little. Even the mass of party members are no longer pulling their full weight in the struggle for production, and recent purges of local officials have been on a scale unprecedented since the Thirties. The faint flicker of post-war optimism has given way to a sort of dreary apathy which has resulted in lowered production. This applies to the U.S.S.R. as a whole. But both unofficial reports and official admissions, oblique or direct, show that in the minority republics, Azerbaijan, Uzbekistan, Kazakhstan and the autonomous Tartar Republic opposition to Kremlin rule has spread to the highest government circles. In the Ukraine, there is still resistance to the Moscow Government.

In a word, Russia is not strong enough to launch an aggressive war for many years to come and, even if she were strong enough, the Russian people are in no fit state to fight one, while many of the minority nationalities would actively revolt. We should never forget that the White Russians and the Ukrainians welcomed the Germans as liberators in the first months of the last war until Hitler showed his true face, while the mass of the ordinary Russians west of the Volga put no heart into the fight until they had experienced for themselves the wickedness of the Nazis.

As far as numbers go, the Red Army could overrun Europe. As

far as armaments and aircraft go, it could swamp Western defenses. This has been true for the past three years. But in view of
retaliation from the air, the potential armed might of the United
States, the shaky state of Soviet morale, and the colossal problems
of holding Europe down by force—as well as the whole of the
U.S.S.R.—that sort of adventure can have few attractions for the
Kremlin.

However, Russia has been an expanding power since the foundation of the Muscovite state in the fourteenth century. This
instinctive expansionism has always been characterized by two pe-
culiarities: a defensive attitude, shot through with a certain mission-
ary zeal, and an easy readiness to stop when it finds itself up
against a firm barrier. These profound Russian characteristics fit
with remarkable exactitude into the Bolshevik theory of action.
Left to herself, Russia would expand right around the globe. The
Czars were hedged in by great powers: Prussia, Austria and Japan.
Stalin is not. But he has America to cope with, which the Czars
did not have, and what is left of the British Empire, which is still
a force.

An extremely important point—indeed, the supremely important point—about this expansionist impulse is that it has been
Russia's ruin in the past and seems likely to be her ruin in the future. By spreading her people and her resources too thinly over
the ground, the governments of Russia have prevented the standard of living, and with it the productivity of the people, from
rising.

But the point we are discussing is whether this lust for space
goes hand in hand with the waging of aggressive war. The answer
is that it does not. The traditional Russian campaign is the spacious defensive campaign, followed by pursuit of an exhausted
enemy.

And this fits in with the Bolshevik philosophy, as outlined not
only by Lenin, but also by Soviet military strategists. Only when
the Bolsheviks are quite sure of easy and overwhelming victory
will they permit themselves to attack openly with guns—as in the
case of the Finnish campaign, which was considered afterward an

error of judgment. And what most people do not seem to realize is that the Soviet Army itself is imbued with this doctrine. In his book, "The Brain of the Army," the Soviet Marshal, Shaposhnikov, makes it quite clear that the enemy is to be defeated by political means before a shot is fired, so that when the troops are finally deployed, all they are required to do is to push over a tottering edifice.

It is plain that this attitude makes perfectly good sense if one is convinced, as the Communists are, that history is on their side; that sooner or later capitalism will collapse under its own weight and as a result of its own internal contradictions, and that all the good Communist has to do is to trust in Marx and keep his powder dry. Sooner or later a clash must come: The supreme objective is to insure that the citadel of communism is in a fit state to profit by it when the day arrives. Soviet Russia, far from being in a fit state to profit by war with the United States and the British Empire, is, as we have seen, not even in a fit state to profit by war with Yugoslavia.

That is why I do not expect the U.S.S.R. to initiate total war for a very long time to come, if ever. Such an onslaught on a strong position has no place in the Leninist-Stalinist philosophy. And the idea of some people that Stalin is going out for world domination as such (as distinct, that is, from presiding, if he is spared, over an expanding Communist empire) will not hold water. According to all of Stalin's teaching, the world revolution is not a steady process, but proceeds in intermittent leaps. The first big leap was in 1917 and after. The second was in 1945 and after. And just as, according to Stalin's own theory of ebb and flow, the capitalist world managed to stabilize itself in the Twenties, so what is left of it will manage to stabilize itself in the Fifties.

Meanwhile, the Kremlin has China to think about. China, which I, personally, see as the beginning of the end of Muscovite power. China will occupy the best brains and resources of the Communist party of the U.S.S.R. for some time to come. The building up of the Soviet Far East, for example, is not at all pure gain to Moscow It is being done at the direct expense of European Russia—just as, in a far lesser but still fatal degree, it was done before in the time of the Czars.

There is one other bogy which worries a great many people. If Stalin feels himself slipping, they say isn't this the very thing to drive him into some wild adventure to divert attention from the shortcomings of the Soviet régime? I see no danger of this at all. In the first place, I do not believe that Stalin is a megalomaniac in the Hitler manner. In the second place, the Russian people for centuries have regarded war as an unmitigated evil.

It is my firm belief that if Stalin plunged his country into war it would be the end of his régime. He knows that his own overthrow was missed only by a hair's breadth in 1941, when innumerable Russians in the West were welcoming the Germans as liberators and when, for a few months, practically the whole nation, even those who fought bravely, saw the Government's failure to keep the country out of war as the ultimate betrayal.

But even if the Kremlin does not want war and will not start one for many years, this does not mean that there will be no war. The Leninist campaign of disruption outside Russia may be so successful and may call for such sustained and concentrated effort to counter it that sooner or later the West may be forced to conclude that it can no longer go on squandering its substance in maintaining a state of constant preparedness for attack. Then it might conceivably be necessary to say to the Russians: "We have so far been containing you, can continue to do so, but the cost is more than we are willing to pay. We are sick of living in an armed camp at the expense of all decent living. If you persist in your absurd and evil course of trying to break us down internally and of tyrannizing over half of Europe we shall have to take decisive action —namely, to wipe you out by means of total war."

This sort of situation, it seems to me, is the only one in which there lies a real danger of war. If the Kremlin continues on its present course and the rest of the world allows it to do so, it will become more probable day by day. But there are many stages between our present passive resistance to Communist expansion and a final ultimatum. And if our statesmen can bring themselves to think aggressively instead of defensively, then there is every chance that we shall be able to do without an ultimatum at all.

But we have to remember that statesmen do not function in a vacuum. They are sustained and upheld by public opinion. With the people in a defeatist frame of mind, our leaders will never get around to thinking aggressively. To produce the suitable mental and emotional climate for a new sort of approach to the Russian problem we have to get back our own nerve and stop being hyp. notized by the sheer vastness of Russia. To do that, we have to take a great deal more trouble to understand both the Soviet Union and communism, their strength and their weakness.

If we do this, we shall be amazed that we have allowed ourselves for so long to be reduced to panic and stampeded into so many retreats. This new mode of exasperated confidence will soon find ways and means of expressing itself in action of a kind that Stalin understands. But without it we are helpless.

A Crusading Faith
to Counter Communism

by Barbara Ward

SHOULD WE NOW despair of peace in our time? President Truman's grim announcement that with the Communist attack on South Korea "communism has passed beyond the use of subversion to conquer independent nations and will now use armed invasion and war" seems to mark the epitaph of any hope of peaceful co-existence of two worlds—the Communist and the free.

The weight of the evidence does, indeed, seem to be on the side of the pessimists for, if history is any guide, once a powerful state becomes the vehicle of a crusading ideal, the most likely outcome is a violent collision with other countries upon which it seeks to impose its crusade. Germany, drunk with the dream of Aryan supremacy, and Italy, carried away by the myth of Rome, have plunged the world into war within this generation. And now, within five years of conquering those evil forces, we face the Soviet Union, prepared apparently by every means to impose the Communist gospel. If this is not the recipe for war, what is?

Happily for our hopes of peace, the analogies of history are not all equally depressing. Since the attack upon South Korea was launched and the United States took the lead in an attempt to repel force by force, it has been pointed out by every commentator that, this time at least, the Western World has not fallen into the trap of appeasement. The quick reaction has served a warning on the aggressors that there will be no repetition of the melancholy retreat which took Europe from the Nazi reoccupation of the Rhineland to the rape of Austria and on to the destruction of Czechoslovakia before the line was finally drawn in Poland.

The record of the Nineteen Thirties is not to be repeated. That is the first and decisive comfort that peace-loving men can draw from history. It is also the most obvious—but there are others, since the division of the Western World between warring faiths is unhappily not new. Catholic and Protestant, Christian and Moslem have, in the past, made Europe, the New World and Asia their ideological battlefields.

The analogies which can be drawn from their struggles may not be exact—no historical analogy can be absolutely accurate—but, equally, they will not be entirely misleading. Two great religious wars have shaken Western civilization—the Moslem attack on Christianity which reached one climax in the Arab conquest of Africa and Spain, and another in the Turkish invasion of the Balkans some seven hundred years later, and the wars of the sixteenth and seventeenth centuries between Catholic and Protestant states. It is possible that the conditions which prevailed then were not so entirely different from those of today. They may, therefore, throw some light upon our modern fear that a world divided between democrats and totalitarians cannot keep the peace.

The earlier wars of religion seem to have passed through four phases. In the first, the existing order of ideas was weakened—by indolence or abuses, by the failure of men to adapt themselves to new forces, by political division and confusion. It was, for instance, in the former Oriental colonies of the Roman Empire that Mohammed claimed to reveal a new and more simple faith and to right the glaring social evils of debt and slavery. There was nothing to resist the spread of Islam in North Africa. It swept through Spain and was only halted by the rising power of the Franks at the Battle of Poitiers in 732 A. D. Then the line came into existence and the Moslems advanced no further.

Similarly, it was the social rigidity and the political collapse of the Orthodox Byzantine Empire that let the Moslem Turks first into Constantinople and then into Europe; their advance continued until they were twice checked by a European coalition of Christian princes before the very gates of Vienna.

Much of the same development accompanied the division of Europe between Catholics and Protestants. Protestantism came in part as a revolt against many signs of corruption and a falling off within the Catholic Church. It established itself most strongly in those lands least permeated with the Roman idea, and, after running strongly for a time through Germany, England, the Low Countries and Scandinavia, and advancing in Austria and France, it came to rest along a line—still observable in Europe today—which it had not the strength to overrun.

The establishment of this line marks the second phase. By using sufficient force in self-defense, the old order brings the march of new ideas to a standstill and creates frontiers. The process may involve some border warfare (such as has occurred in our own day in Greece), but once the line of advance is clearly fixed and the crusaders of the new faith recognize that their opponents will give no further ground, the frontiers tend to become established. This process is accelerated and confirmed by the third phase, in which the old order—Christian Europe menaced by the Moslems, Catholic Europe hard pressed by Protestantism—takes stock of its own weaknesses, failures and divisions and undergoes a process of renewal.

In the sixth and seventh centuries the emergence of an organized state power in France and the empire building of Charlemagne owed something to the pressure of the Moslems from the south, while that remarkable political achievement of Central Europe— the multi-national empire of the Habsburgs—came into being almost solely to preserve Europe from the attacks of the Turks in the fifteenth and sixteenth centuries. The same process was observable within the Catholic community as a result of the Protestant challenge Many of the reforms for which reformers had pressed came about after the Council of Trent and the Counter-Reformation was a time of spiritual and cultural revival throughout the Catholic world.

This phase of renewal has a double importance, since it is doubtful whether frontiers first established by successful military defenses could be held if revived faith and renewed political and cultural vitality did not come to reinforce the old order. Successful defense and internal renewal seem to be part of the same process, and certainly in our own day—in China, indeed, within a year —the consequence of relying on military resources unsupported by any political or moral reserve has been collapse and defeat.

In the last phase of all the clear-cut frontier itself begins to fade. Two forces may come in time—and by reason of some new danger that menaces them both—to tolerate each other, and even to begin a process of rapprochement. Such seems to be the present state of Catholicism and Protestantism. Or else the old crusading faith of the aggressor slackens; its political and economic arteries harden; it produces its own version of tyranny and finally falls away, defeated by the renewed strength and confidence of the system it once attacked. This was the fate of the Moslem incursion into Europe.

So much for history. Has it anything to tell us about the present divisions and about the possible co-existence—in peace—of the two rival systems of our modern world? In some respects, the fifth and fifteenth centuries seem so remote from us that it is hard to believe their experience relevant. But is the sequence of events so different today? Communism is certainly the child of failures and weaknesses in the Western World. Who have had least cause to realize the benefits of Western democracy? It is the mass of workingmen, particularly in Europe and in the new industrial nations of Asia. It is also the subject peoples in the colonies, whose national feeling has stoked the fires of economic discontent. We need not, therefore, be surprised that among these groups communism is strong today and—in Southeast Asia—may grow stronger.

Nor has communism simply exploited the discontent of the masses. Among a certain intellectual élite, it is again the failures of Western society that have made converts to Marxism. The weaknesses of a Christianity that could not redeem the crude exploitation of early industrialism; the instabilities of an economic system that could produce great riches and yet periodically—with the rise and fall of the trade cycle—fail to distribute them; the long misery of mass unemployment—these were the evils that drove young spirits and generous minds to embrace communism.

We can, therefore, say that the Western World has already repeated the first phase of the earlier wars of religion. The failures and weaknesses of the old order have nourished the aggressive faith of the new crusade. But the comparison is much less certain for the following phases—first, the fixing of the line upon which the crusaders are checked, if necessary by force, and then the renewal and reinvigoration of the Western way of life.

The decision of the free nations to withstand aggression in Korea is, of course, the first and essential step toward the fixing of a firm line containing Communist expansion. Notice has been served on the Russians—as it was never served until too late upon the Nazis—that any attempt to cross the present frontiers of the non-Communist world by force will be resisted, and will, if pressed home, lead to a general war. The very remoteness of Korea from the main field of Western interests is an added reminder to the Communists that it is aggression as such, and not a narrow view of their own interests, that compels the Western powers to make their stand.

The line has thus been drawn. Doubts arise when one considers the means available to defend it, and the seriousness of Western intentions in making their defense effort a first priority in all their planning. The most vulnerable front is still Western Europe. So long as it is virtually certain that Russian armies can occupy Europe's Western fringe, the whole Western capacity for checking aggression anywhere is in jeopardy. If Russian forces attack directly in any part of the world, the way to check them is by striking back at the Soviet Union itself. But if the Soviet retort is an instant occupation of Europe, the West will hesitate to act. First priority in holding a world-wide line is thus an effective system of defense in Europe, not within three years but within six months. Is Western planning and preparedness geared to such an effort? If not, the lesson of Korea will be lost.

Even graver doubts are raised by the third phase apparent in the old wars of religion—the stage at which the culture or community under attack draws together its own resources and releases a new wave of reforming zeal and energy within its own society. Are we in the West showing much sign of this? There are two problems here: first, the achievement of just, dynamic and prosperous conditions in our own advanced Western society, and, second, and almost certainly more difficult, the discovery of the version of our society which is appreciable to the more backward peoples of Asia. The line in Asia is, after all, as much menaced by the internal revolt of the people against their old rulers and bad conditions as by direct attack from without. As we have seen in the Chinese, the problem of holding the line and of renewing the social order can be almost identical. If the Formosans, the Indo-Chinese, the Filipinos, the peasants of Malaya and Indonesia and the masses of India see nothing before them but poverty, illiteracy and dependence upon landlords and tribal chiefs, then communism, with its promises of liberation, land reform, modernization and advance may not need to attack openly. It can successfully bore from within.

What can we say of ourselves in this context? There are, it is true, some stirrings of awareness that the successful withstanding of communism's world crusade entails more than lip service to the ideal of international cooperation or to the coordination of diplomatic moves to counter Soviet strategy. The Marshall Plan has succeeded in restoring European production; under its aegis the powers of Europe's Western fringe are feeling their way cautiously in the matter of closer integration. A few individuals speak of an Atlantic Union. Some attempt is being made to consider what will be done to hold the West together when the Marshall Plan comes to an end. But it cannot be said that there is any real quickening of life and initiative. On the contrary, the average citizen is bewildered by endless talk of payments schemes, plans for heavy industry and liberalization of trade. Objectives are too detailed, political vision too dim to give him life or heart.

The outlook for Asia seems even less promising. The British Commonwealth is at work preparing a project of economic assistance. President Truman's Point Four has aroused enthusiasm in the world—but not in Congress. A certain amount of spade work on technical assistance is going on in the United Nations. Some individual steps have been taken. For instance, Gen. Douglas MacArthur, by pressing through land reform in Japan, has destroyed one of the most fruitful sources of communism in Asia—peasant discontent. But no statesman in the East or West has a really very clear picture of how, under modern conditions, the newly independent governments of Asia can be given the guidance and assistance they need so that they will not fall prey to internal, Communist-backed disintegration. All plans for economic aid move at snail's pace, discontent with the speed of light.

These uncertainties over Western policy are all the more tragic in that there is at least a possibility that Soviet Russia may enter a phase of rigidity, conservatism and decay rather more rapidly than some of the earlier crusaders of European history. That the Russians are still capable of vast economic expansion is no doubt true. What they may be losing is the power of appealing to the world's idealism or of offering an attractive alternative to the Western way of life.

The powers of a police state, the farce of Soviet justice, ruthless collectivization of unwilling peasants, the drudgery and regimentation of workers are better known than they were ten or even five years ago. The fact of naked aggression is beginning to make nonsense of their peace campaign. A vast revulsion against tyranny may yet sweep the world, provided only that the Western powers meanwhile preserve and renew their own social fabric. The lesson of history is, after all, a simple one—that though force can and must be checked by force, faith alone can counter faith.

If communism and democracy are to survive in the same world, the pre-condition is such a reassertion of military strength and such a strengthening of political freedom in the West, so ambitious a scale of economic progress for the whole non-Communist world, and so keen a revival of personal faith in the Western way of life that a free society can become once again the center of the world's hopes. The program may seem sweeping, the effort immense. But—another lesson of history—crusading ideas cannot be countered without an effort equal to their own.

"To Save Humanity from the Deep Abyss"

by John Foster Dulles

ON JUNE 25, 1950, darkness settled on the world. Only one thing was clear; that was the path of duty. Where it might lead us was obscure.

On that Sunday morning the Republic of Korea was violently attacked. Along its entire northern border planes, tanks and artillery poured out of their hidden concentrations to assault the youngest member of the free world. They destroyed not only lives and homes but also the twin illusions that communism loves peace and is hostile only to nations which are socially diseased.

The Republic of Korea was a healthy society. That I had learned first-hand on a visit which immediately preceded the criminal assault. The republic had just held its second general election. Over 80 per cent of the eligible voters had gone to the polls. There were vigorous contests for every seat and a majority of the representatives elected were independent of the Syngman Rhee party, which constitutionally controlled the machinery of Government.

From the *New York Times Magazine*, July 30, 1950, copyright © 1950 by The New York Times Company.

That in itself proved the reality of political freedom and disproved the allegations of "political terrorism."

We spent an unforgettable evening in religious worship with 3,000 Christian refugees who had fled from the terrorism of North Korea to enjoy the religious liberty of the Republic of Korea. The hymns and prayers of the assembled multitude bore eloquent testimony to the existence in the Republic of Korea of religious liberty. We met with educational leaders, both those charged with elementary education and university leaders charged with higher education. They had hopeful plans, already being realized, for making educational opportunities generally available for the alert and eager minds of the Korean youth.

The Korean women were active in this educational field and also in politics. Two women had been elected to the National Legislature. To an extent unusual in East Asia, there was realization of the United Nations goal of "equal rights of men and women."

We talked with economic and business leaders, official and private, Korean and foreign. The economy of the country was rapidly improving under the impact of hard work. United States economic aid was scheduled to end in 1952. Already, in the current year, 100,000 tons of rice had been set aside for export to Japan, as part of an exchange which would relieve the economic burden of the United States in relation both to Japan and Korea.

Extensive land reforms were under way. When Korea was liberated, 70 per cent of the farm families were tenants and only 30 per cent were owners. Already the percentage of owners had been increased to 55 per cent and plans scheduled for this summer would have raised the owners to 90 per cent.

We saw the republic's army and police force and talked with United States military advisers. It was their unqualified testimony that the morale, loyalty and discipline were of the highest, although there was concern because the army did not possess a single combat plane or tank or artillery heavy enough to stop opposing tanks.

All in all, the Republic of Korea was conducting a promising experiment in democracy. That was the opinion of the United States Embassy in Korea, of the members of the United Nations Korean Commission and of the members of the diplomatic corps. The British Minister, now unhappily a prisoner, told me that he had seen, in many parts of the world, experiments in the development of self-government. Never, he said, had he seen progress as rapid and solid as that being made by the Republic of Korea.

Of course, everything was not perfect. That was scarcely to be expected. But at least the society was sufficiently wholesome so that communism could not conquer it from within. For two years that had been tried by Korean Communists infiltrated from the North and the attempts had failed dismally. The Republic of Korea had been tested and found not vulnerable to subversive tactics such as had succeeded, or offered chance of success, in other parts of Asia. This Korean experiment in democracy—this moral salient in the otherwise solid Communist despotism of North Asia—could be destroyed, if at all, only by the brutal method of open armed aggression. So that was tried.

We now see that when a society is good enough to be impervious to indirect aggression, it is not on that account safe. It then has to face the menace of direct aggression. What happened in Korea proves that the Bolshevik Communist leaders are contemptuous of the moral principles and aspirations which drew the people of the world together to form the United Nations.

As the preamble to the United Nations Charter sets out, the United Nations was the act of peoples who had faith in fundamental human rights and in the dignity and worth of the human person; who recognized that this requires tolerance and restraint of violence, so that force shall be used only in the common interest. That is why "We the Peoples of the United Nations . . . have resolved to combine our efforts."

Article 2 of the Charter establishes the principle that "all members shall refrain in their international relations from the threat or use of force against the territorial integrity or political independence of any state" and that non-member nations also must act in accordance with this rule. And Article 56 pledges the members "to take joint and separate action in cooperation with the organization" to promote "universal respect for, and observance of, human rights and fundamental freedoms for all."

The free world had hoped that these principles, backed by the potential power of those who held them, would prevent open aggression. Our Government authorized me to support that hope in Korea. We knew that the Communist puppet Government of North Korea was emboldened, and the people of the republic were fearful, because the republic was not a member of the United Nations, having been prevented from joining by a Soviet veto. Also, the republic was not protected by any security pact, such as the North Atlantic and Rio pacts. We thought that it would be salutary to recall publicly in Korea that the republic, even though deprived of formal membership in any organization for peace, was nevertheless the beneficiary of the universal principles and moral compulsions that undergirded the United Nations and bound together the free world.

So, on the invitation of the Korean Second National Assembly, I addressed its opening session. I concluded with these paragraphs, written before I left Washington:

> The United Nations considers you as, spiritually, one of them. The members acted with near unanimity to advance your political freedom and to seek your unity with the north. And today even though you are technically deprived of formal membership by Russian veto, nevertheless the United Nations requires all nations to refrain from any threat or use of force against your territorial integrity or political independence.
>
> In addition, there is what we call the "Free World." The Free World has no written Charter, but it is no less real for that. Membership depends on the conduct of a nation itself; there is no veto. Its compulsions to common action are powerful, because they flow from a profound sense of common destiny.
>
> The American people welcome you as an equal partner in

the great company of those who make up this Free World, a world which commands vast moral and material power and resolution that is unswerving. That power and that determination combine to assure that any despotism which wages aggressive war dooms itself to unutterable disaster.

Therefore, I say to you: You are not alone. You will never be alone so long as you continue to play worthily your part in the great design of human freedom.

Those words of hope to the republic, and of warning to the northern despotism, were broadcast into all Korea, north and south. They did not, unhappily, prevent the attack which, we now see, had been long planned. Within six days the Republic was struck with armed force and the United States declaration was quickly put to the test. It stood up. The United Nations Security Council met within twenty-four hours of the attack and, in the light of a cabled report from its own commission in Korea, unhesitatingly branded the attack as a breach of the peace and called upon the member states for assistance.

Two days later President Truman acted promptly and vigorously, with bipartisan support, to bring the United States to respond to that appeal and the governments of fifty-two other nations have now evidenced their support. What happened showed that, in truth, there is within the Free World a "profound sense of common destiny," so that when any part is attacked the "compulsions to common action are powerful."

It is imperative that these "compulsions" should now find adequate expression. Their adequacy must be measured by the assumption that the Bolshevik Communist leaders are willing now to accept greatly increased risks of war, in order to achieve their purposes. If that were not so they would not have permitted this deliberate attack on Korea. They must have believed that, in case of need, their superior military force-in-being would enable them to gain initial victories which would so strengthen them and weaken the free world that despotism would have a good chance to win eventual victory.

Within the last year the Soviet Union has completed tanks and combat planes in vast numbers, exceeding by many times the total of military planes and tanks available to the free world. It is not usual for a nation, particularly one of relative poverty, to turn its steel and aluminum into actual military equipment which is subject to rapid depreciation and obsolescence unless it thinks that the military equipment may be needed for use before it depreciates or becomes obsolete.

We see now at least part of that use, as Soviet-manufactured tanks and planes carry death to the defenders of the Korean Republic. Also we know that the Soviet-manufactured armor which penetrates into South Korea taps only slightly the vast armament reservoir that has been created in the center of the Eurasian land mass.

Since international communism may not be deterred by moral principles backed by *potential* might, we must back those principles with military strength-in-being, and do so quickly. That is our national determination, voiced by President Truman, on July 19, 1950, in his messages to the people and the Congress. The grave question is whether we shall be able to create this strength in time to change what may be the war calculations of international communism.

It was inevitable that a critical moment would come when international communism felt that it had exhausted most of the possibilities of gain through methods of indirect aggression. It had, through these methods, won and consolidated great victories in central and southeastern Europe and in Asia. However, the free world was visibly checking the possibilities of further big gains by indirect aggression.

The European Recovery Plan, the North Atlantic Pact, the Military Aid Program and the Schuman steel pool proposal had led to a revival of hope and vigor in Western Europe. Communist strength there has been sharply declining. In Asia, the United States had turned from what had seemed to be a policy of drift and we were in the process of developing positive policies which would give leadership and hope to the Asiatic forces opposed to communism. Thus, the free world was ending the possibilities of indirect aggression.

While this was going on, the Soviet Union was creating a vast supply of tanks and planes to equip both the armies of the Soviet Union and also the Soviet-trained and officered armies of the satellite states. Now, the Communist regime of North Korea has struck with armed might.

The combination of these developments may mark a new phase of Bolshevik Communist aggression. It may invalidate the assumption that the Soviet Union would not risk general war for several years yet to come—the time presumably required for it to develop a large stockpile of atomic weapons. It surely invalidates the assumption that we can continue still for a time to live luxuriously, without converting our economic potential into military reality.

The present consequence of that past assumption is that the free world is only meagerly equipped to check the offensive power of Communist satellite armies, quite apart from the armies of the Soviet Union itself. The situation is precarious. It need not yet be assumed that general war is inevitable, but any further armed aggression would seriously strain the whole fabric of peace.

We have said that the leaders of Soviet communism seem now willing to run greatly increased risks of war. That, however, does not necessarily mean that they *want* general war or that they are irrevocably committed to provoke it. The free world, perhaps, may still bring the Soviet leaders to avoid that reckless course. The best chance is for the free members of the United Nations to present a solid, cohesive unity and to demonstrate that they have both the resolution to defend the high principles of the Charter and also the willingness to accept sacrifice and discipline so that their resolution may be potent unto the end.

The United States, which produces five times as much steel as the Soviet Union, has been using for military purposes less than half as much steel as does the Soviet Union. If we had used, for military purposes, twice as much steel as does the Soviet Union, our people would still have had for their enjoyment four times as much steel as is available to the Russian people. The picture is similar for aluminum, oil and other key commodities.

Communist leaders may understandably have doubted our devotion to the principles we verbally espouse when we have seemed so negligent of the means to defend them.

The time for sacrifice and discipline is here. In fact it has been here for long, but it took the attack on Korea to open our eyes. Many now will risk their lives before the hard battle of Korea is won. Most of us will have to work longer hours and with more intensity. We shall have to give up some material enjoyments and be more frugal in our living. There will be fewer automobiles, television sets and gadgets to buy and there will be bigger tax bills to pay.

Despite all that, I predict that we shall not, as a nation, be less happy. There is never great happiness in leading a purposeless life, whether in poverty or in richness. We have, as a nation, been blessed with fabulous material prosperity; but we have too much been purposeless and without sense of dedication or of mission.

Now we are consciously enlisted in a great cause. We have enlisted voluntarily, as befits free men and women, and we sacrifice voluntarily. We do not work and sacrifice as slaves to any master save truth and righteousness. Our purpose is to join our strength with that of the other free members of the United Nations to preserve such human liberty as remains in the world and to extend liberty by gradually releasing the captive peoples.

We are engaged in the kind of crusade that Lincoln foresaw when he said, of our Declaration of Independence, that it promised "liberty, not alone to the people of this country, but hope for the world for all future time."

We are determined to wage our cause peacefully so far as that is humanly possible because we know that the destructions and cruelties of war themselves breed despotism and intolerance. The war in Korea was not of our making and we can still be hopeful that it can be confined and extinguished so as to prevent a general war.

If that awful cataclysm impends, it is primarily because the Bolshevik Communist leaders have gravely miscalculated the resolution and the willingness to sacrifice of the free peoples. It is our task to correct that miscalculation before the consequences are irreparable. That is a matter of deeds, not words alone.

If the free peoples act quickly, largely and unitedly to translate their freedom into strength of moral purpose and material might, they may yet save humanity from the deep abyss. Let that be our dedication.

Part 2

A TIME OF TESTING

THE KOREAN WAR subjected American leaders to a series of temptations. First was the temptation to let the cup pass, abandon South Korea to the Communists, and fall back to prepared strong points. General MacArthur was not alone in his surprise that Truman and Acheson did not succumb to that course he thought repugnant. After all, the Joint Chiefs had advised against becoming enmeshed in a Korean civil war, no matter what its causes. For a time, then, MacArthur and the administration were united in purpose, but after the General's almost miraculous breakout from the Pusan perimeter, a new temptation arose: the urge to "liberate" North Korea.

MacArthur's hubris drove the General to commit tactical errors (he flew to Pyongyang on October 20, 1950, demanding to know upon his arrival if there were "any celebrities here to greet me? Where's Kim Buck Too?"), but it was not the force that led civilian policy-makers astray. MacArthur's drive to the Manchurian border was fully supported by Washington. Years afterward, former Secretary of State Dean Acheson would comment: "MacArthur was a jackass. 'f he'd done what he had been told to do, the war would have been finished early, but he wanted to be spectacular, and he loused it up." To credit this statement as the final word on Chinese intervention, one must also credit the new leaders of that country with unbelievable restraint and forbearance. There is no way to make the General pay for all the mistakes of the Korean War. But Truman and Acheson did resist the temptation to back MacArthur in new adventures on the Chinese frontier, or to flout atomic threats. The articles in this section trace the rapidly changing attitudes in the United States as the war moved from "containment" to "liberation" and back again.

Hanson Baldwin and Peggy Durdin tried to put Korea into the context of Asia's strategic "rimlands," and warned of the "atmosphere of impending storm which seems to hang over Asia. . . ." Nathaniel Peffer reminded Americans that the first priority for defense was still Europe. George F. Kennan advised the reader not to get carried away in an emotional reaction to the Chinese intervention. Even granting that the Chinese government was in the hands of excited and irresponsible people, he wrote: "They are not the first people that we have known that were that way, and they will not be the last; and we are not the keepers of their souls."

In a "Memorandum" to General MacArthur, columnist James Reston suggested that the pre-war isolationist-interventionist debate had shrunk to a political squabble, that all the Republican furor over Far Eastern policy was simply pre-election tactics, and that (by implication) the General should not take too seriously his chances for building a grass-roots movement against administration foreign policy.

Journey into War
—New York to Korea

by W. H. Lawrence

KOREA.

ON A MAP the journey from the eastern seaboard of the United States to Korea is about 7,000 miles. It took me, all told, ten days. The traveler who goes from the one territory to the other sees two entirely different worlds—a world of production, safety and enjoyment of life and a world of destruction, danger and struggle for existence. The first is such a world as all mankind could attain if human problems were solved by mutual endeavor; the other is the bitter consequence of dictatorship.

For this correspondent, fresh from the politics-as-usual (or even worse-than-usual) atmosphere of the recent South Carolina primary election, another contrast is apparent between these two worlds: a contrast of the unworthy and the finest moments of democracy. In Carolina two men fought for a seat in the United States Senate, offering as their principal qualification the ability to uphold white supremacy and oppose the program of the President of the United States. Here in Korea white, black and yellow men,

From the *New York Times Magazine*, August 6, 1950, copyright © 1950 by The New York Times Company.

under the direction of the same President, are fighting and dying to uphold the principle that men of whatever color should be free to govern themselves in a democratic society and not be subject to a totalitarian communism imposed by force of arms.

The journey westward from the comforts of American civilization to the front line of Korea gradually prepares a traveler for the ordeal of war. One has a sense of increasing tension and increasing responsibility each day of this trip west across America, north to Alaska, over the Pacific to Tokyo and on toward the shelling and bombing and blood and mud of the Korean front.

I started the journey with the harsh words of Senator Olin D. Johnston and Governor J. Strom Thurmond in the South Carolina Senatorial battle ringing in my ears. In Washington I encountered the first change of atmosphere; the capital, in the two weeks I had been away from it, had dropped much of its customary politics. Although there still were some irritating political traces, the sprawling apparatus of government seemed, in general, to have acquired a sense of purpose. There was less lost motion and a new determination to get a difficult job accomplished.

But Washington still was a long way from the war. Never had the sky seemed so blue or Rock Creek Park, through the center of the city, so green as on the morning I finally had to say good-by and head off to my third shooting war (the Pacific and Greece had come before) in less than five years. It was a hard thing to say farewell to the pretty girl driving me to the airport; it would have been so much pleasanter to whip down the top of the convertible and drive off to the lakes of New Hampshire, but the war of the United Nations against aggression has to be reported as well as fought.

In New York, the next point on the way, the echoes of war were muted by the bustle of the millions of people. There was, of course, talk of the struggle far away, but the talk had a quality of remoteness from reality. There was more vigorous talk, it seemed, about what the Yankees were doing and whether the Dodgers had at long last caught fire and might be headed for the top of the heap in the National League pennant race.

By mid-evening, after departure from New York, I could look far down from the Northwest Airlines Stratocruiser upon the green fields of the Middle West, where the wheat was almost ready for harvesting and the corn was growing taller. The passengers talked of the war: "How long will it last?" "Will the Russians get into it openly?" No one had satisfactory answers, and again the questions seemed far away from the reality of the ripening fields below.

Near midnight the airplane touched down at Seattle. The city was asleep except in the area of the great Boeing aircraft plant, where new calls for labor have been going out daily to step up the production of B-50's for the Air Force. The docks were crowded with ships ready to move westward. Some of the shipyards were increasing their tempo of work. One had called that day for more welders to turn out new ships, possibly to be ready to repair damaged vessels.

Here the war was 3,000 miles closer. The few persons with whom I had the opportunity to talk during the brief stopover seemed well satisfied that the President had acted quickly and courageously in calling the bluff of international communism. There was no saber rattling, simply a quiet determination to find out whether man could live in peace without the threat of armed aggression. They were ready for whatever calls the President and Congress might make, but wanted him to tell the nation the cold, hard facts of life and get ready for an all-out struggle.

From Seattle, in the morning, the airplane turned north non-stop across the rugged mountains of Canada toward Alaska, our first line of defense if the Russians should attempt an invasion from the north across the narrow Bering Straits. The stop at Anchorage lasts only an hour and the traveler is isolated from the general public, since the plane lands at a military field.

Here one sees the nearness of the war for the first time. As the aircraft settled down on the runway I noticed that all anti-aircraft batteries were manned and that a line of swift, sleek jet fighters were hooked up to generators, ready to jump into the air on a minute's notice.

Already some of the wounded from Korea are on their way

home, and the traveler observes military censorship for the first time. Notice is handed to all returning veterans of Korea urging them to use restraint in answering queries from the press. The final two paragraphs are interesting: "No implication should be made further than the fact that our nation is engaged in executing the desires of the United Nations in order to bring Communist aggression to a halt and to preserve the stability of the Orient until such time as international agreements concerning the area may be made for the future.

"Aggression is defined as being committed by the North Korean Communist forces. Statements or implications to the effect that any other nation or group of nations is being combatted by United States forces are unauthorized."

An overnight flight including a ticklish landing at fog-bound Chemya in the Aleutian chain finally brings the traveler over Tokyo at 9 A. M. In the early hours of the morning the city presents a picture differing greatly from the first and last times I had previously seen it.

On that first trip, April 13, 1945, Tokyo time—the same day that President Roosevelt died—I had ridden north with Guam-based B-29's to give Tokyo its second dose of liquid, flaming petroleum. Coming over the target in the last wave of attacking planes just before midnight, I looked down on eleven square miles of flame. Hunks of metal hurled skyward by anti-aircraft guns banged into the plane, damaging it slightly.

The last time I had seen Tokyo was shortly after the Japanese surrendered, in September of the same year, when more than sixty miles of the city were in ruins. As I flew over the city on the present trip I found that the Japanese had effaced most of the scars of bombing.

The stopover in Tokyo lasted only six hours, because I was lucky enough to find an empty seat on an Air Force courier plane headed for a southern Japanese air base, a jumping-off point for Korea. But while I was in the bustling streets of Tokyo I had no awareness that the war was only about 800 miles away. A greater danger to life and limb arose from the mad antics of the Japanese auto drivers.

At the air base in southern Japan the good luck that had brought me from New York in little more than three days ran out. Typhoons had been playing around the southern part of Japan and Korea for several days; flying conditions were impossible. But while waiting for transport I saw the most convincing answer to the racial appeals of the Carolina politicians. An ambulance plane from the Korean front, allowed to take off because of the urgency of its errand, rolled to a stop on the airstrip where Red Cross ambulances were lined up. The walking wounded came out.

The first man off the plane was a big Negro rifleman with a patch over one eye. Then a sandy-haired white man wearing a crucifix and clutching his wounded arm. There were several others, black and white, and then the litter patients, about equally divided. Here they were united in the bond of sacrifice, suffering and fighting in a battle so that some yellow men could rule themselves. It was a far cry from the rantings of Johnston and Thurmond on the theme that only white men were fit to rule and that Negroes must always play a subordinate role to a white master.

Soon after the wounded landed word came that we could hitch a ride if we liked on an L. S. T. sailing that night from a near-by port with supplies for the advanced Air Force headquarters in Korea. Hastily rounding up supplies and dry rations for two or three meals, six correspondents hurried to the vessel. It flew no flag and was manned by Japanese who only five years before were the enemies who held Korea in bondage. The voyage across the Sea of Japan was smooth.

We left the L. S. T. at the Pusan harbor entrance when a pilot came aboard and commented jokingly that here, at least, was a country which we could enter without customs formalities. A troop train was ready to leave for the north within an hour after we arrived, and the colonel commanding a military police detachment asked us to share the officers' car. It was furnished with plain hardwood benches, but it was clean.

A bright sun beat down from a clear, blue sky as the train rolled toward the battle lines. It ran swiftly up a narrow green valley between gorge-scarred mountains. The scenery, I thought, reminded me a lot of the Shenandoah Valley. The resemblance stopped where nature's work ended, because the Koreans had built themselves thatched shack after shack amid dirt and squalor which would make any pineboard shack in the Hoovervilles of 1932 look like the Waldorf-Astoria.

At the first water stop a group of thirty Korean school children, waving Korean, American and United Nations flags, lined up beside the track, singing the Korean national anthem. A youngster who could not have been more than 6 gravely conducted them with the dignity of a Toscanini. G. I.'s crowded off the train to take pictures and give candy and chewing gum to the kids. If there was one sour note, it was the suggestion of a veteran of the European campaigns who thought it all a plot to get us off the train while other Koreans entered from the other side and stole our belongings. He was wrong, of course.

That night we bedded down at advance headquarters and suddenly the talk of war was transformed into realistic details of a dozen small actions going on within the hour. In the early hours of the next day, with other correspondents, I set off by jeep for the part of the front line held by the famed First Cavalry Division, which is now a mechanized infantry division and which is proud of its Pacific record—"first in Manila, first in Tokyo."

We drove along narrow roads and around hairpin turns along a series of mountain ranges going north. These roads, never good in the first place and unsuitable for two-lane traffic, were taking a terrible beating from heavy American equipment moving toward the front. The inability of big vehicles to pass one another created traffic jams which held up traffic for hundreds of yards.

During the day I saw several vehicles that ventured too close to the road shoulders and tumbled off the road. The traffic kicked up considerable dust, but some daredevil G. I. drivers gunned their jeeps into it with small concern for their own or others' safety.

In fact, our jeep late in the day had to swerve sharply to avoid another jeep coming down the road in a thick dust cloud, and we plunged twelve feet down an embankment. None of us was hurt.

After driving a few hours (it is impossible to mention distances or towns, for the sake of military security) we came at last to division headquarters, where we found Maj. Gen. Hobart R. Gay. Between trips to the front he was downing a cup of tea in the shade outside his trailer.

A veteran of two world wars and one previous police action (against Mexican bandits), Gay obviously didn't like his present role—that of defensive action. He promised he would strike back at the enemy as soon as possible, because he had not been taught to fight defensive wars and did not propose to learn at this late stage.

Enemy tanks were loose between his division and the adjoining Twenty-fifth Division, and he was giving instructions as to how they were to be cleaned out—by dynamite, if necessary. We asked whether we could proceed toward the front.

"Sure, you can get up there," he replied. "You may get shot at, of course, but you can go on up to Yongdong."

A jeep driver in the courtyard advised us to turn left at the first forked road, avoiding the right turn, because that was where the enemy tanks were loose and attempting to encircle our forward positions.

Weaving our way through traffic, we headed down the road to Yongdong. Up forward we could hear the sound of our artillery firing at enemy positions. As we neared Yongdong we saw trucks ahead make sudden stops and G. I.'s clambered out to take cover behind a high embankment. The enemy was shelling the area. We hit the dirt along with the soldiers.

The small group we were with had never heard a gun fired in anger before, but in a very few minutes they realized the seriousness of war and how close it could strike. While huddling at the sides of the road, they saw a jeep carrying toward the rear the body of their lieutenant, who had been killed in action within a few minutes after shelling started. One of them sitting near us was Cpl. Russell Harrison, a 27-year-old, tall, lithe veteran from Red Bank, N. J., who had served with the Navy in the Pacific war, participating in the Marshalls, Admiralties and Philippines campaigns.

Why had he left the Navy and joined the Army, we wanted to know.

'I just thought I'd like a change," he replied, with a grin. "Guess I got it."

Just about that time General Gay drove by, headed toward the front, and one G. I. commented: "The brass sure is getting up close in this war."

It is safe to say that the generals have made more friends among G. I.'s in the short time Americans have been fighting here than at any time in recent history. They have been up in the thick of action constantly, and—as this article is written—one of them, Maj. Gen. William F. Dean, is still missing in action. He stayed behind with the rear guard covering the evacuation of Taejon, and was seen firing a bazooka personally at enemy tanks. The G. I.'s comment that this is not the kind of job which two-star generals ordinarily undertake personally.

When there was a lull in the firing we made our way forward to an artillery position which was slamming shells into enemy columns detected from the air by observers flying slow, unarmed L-5s, which are similar to the Piper Cubs flown by sportsmen in the States.

Up at the front our artillery is known as "outgoing mail"; the enemy's is known as "incoming mail." For those at home who have been concerned about the reduction in postal service to one residential delivery per day, let it be noted that the G. I.'s here would be glad to settle for one delivery daily of this particular kind of mail.

While we stood there the enemy got some tanks loose to the south of us and we shifted some of our guns to fire south, while other batteries poured the main fire into the principal enemy concentration on the north. Incoming mail was being sent from three directions, and we had to drop to the ground occasionally to avoid flying shrapnel.

A hundred yards or so west of us a G. I. didn't get down fast enough and shrapnel slashed into his shoulder. His young buddy, with tears in his eyes, came to the position where we were squatting and requested transportation. There wasn't an ambulance in the immediate vicinity, so we sent our driver back down the road to pick up our jeep and volunteered to take the wounded man back to an aid station.

By the time the jeep returned, however, there was an ambulance there and the wounded man had been loaded aboard.

It had been five years since I stood with forward artillery positions on Okinawa, but I discovered quickly that the sound of gunfire hadn't grown any more pleasant in the intervening period. At first, our small group of correspondents jumped and ducked at every sound, whether it was the outgoing or incoming fire. The shelling continued for perhaps half an hour.

Returning to the regimental command post to get information on the infantry positions menaced by the tanks, which potentially could cut them off, we found General Gay. He was directing new dispositions of our forces to avoid encirclement. The man who had commanded in Europe with numerous divisions at his disposal now was talking in terms of what to do with single companies. We asked him a few questions and he replied in monosyllables. When we left he was staring moodily in the direction of the enemy lines.

As we drove down the road the sound of firing gradually became faint, the instinct of self-preservation became less dominant and my mind turned back to comparing this—my first experience in the field—with my last domestic assignment in the United States. With disgust I recalled the terribly low level struck by both candidates for Senator from South Carolina.

It seemed hardly possible that the same country in which such appeals for high office could be made also furnished these black and white men I had seen fighting and dying and suffering together so that the yellow men could be free to run their own lives. A song from my favorite musical, "South Pacific," furnished a partial clue: "You've got to be taught to hate."

These kids obviously had not been taught to hate each other or anybody else for that matter. A few more days of combat would give them the bitter incentive to kill their North Korean enemies. But the common sacrifice and suffering they are enduring should keep them from ever hating each other over the circumstance that one has a skin of different color from another.

The New Pattern
of Soviet Aggression

by M. S. Handler

BELGRADE.

THE SOVIET DELEGATION to the United Nations Assembly is attempting to maneuver the Western Governments into an attitude of appeasement. This is a Communist assessment of Soviet Foreign Minister Andrei Vishinsky's sudden display of amiability in face of the military reverses suffered by the North Korean armies.

From a practical point of view, the Soviet leaders are trying to probe the sentiment of the Western Governments to determine whether the time is ripe to resort to the classical maneuver of retreating one step in order to advance two steps at the propitious moment.

The problem facing the Soviet leaders is to determine whether enough pacifist sentiment and capacity for self-delusion is still present in the West to make it possible to draw the Western Governments into complicated negotiations, which would end in their

From the *New York Times Magazine*, October 1, 1950, copyright © 1950 by The New York Times Company.

surrender or gain time for another blow in furtherance of the new Soviet policy of armed aggression.

There is enough evidence to prove that the Soviet has substituted a policy of force for political warfare in order to establish its domination. Partial failure of this new policy in Korea does not mean that the Soviet Government is prepared to spare the use of force. From the Communist point of view, it would mean a temporary reverse which must be rectified by tortuous negotiations.

The purpose of such negotiations would be twofold. The first objective would be to pave the way for eventual political control of all Korea. The second would be to lull the Western Governments into the belief that the Soviet Government has been so frightened that it is prepared to replace armed aggression with diplomacy. This illusion would enable the Soviet Government to continue with its aggressive plans in other parts of the world. Soviet plans for Germany, Austria and against Yugoslavia are a standing reminder of the true nature of Moscow's ambitions.

The Korean attack was a callous exposure of the policy which the Soviet leaders began to develop in late 1943 and early 1944. The consolidation of the Moscow dictatorship during the period of successful defensive war against the Wehrmacht and the beginning of the westward offensive by the Red Army made it necessary for the Soviet leaders to redefine the respective roles to be played by the Red Army and the non-Soviet Communist parties in the liberation of non-Soviet Europe. A new doctrine was born, reversing the respective roles of the army and these Communist parties in the movement for a world revolution.

Prior to the complete emergence of the new policy the Soviet method of operation was based on Lenin's concept that each foreign Communist party could and would make its own revolution. Toward this end the function of the Presidium of the Comintern, which sat in Moscow, was to plan and coordinate various moves in each foreign country for the purpose of stimulating the revolution. And although the betrayal of the German Communist party to the Nazis in 1932 was the first indication that the Communist party of the Soviet Union, under Stalin's control, was changing its line and role, the foreign Communist parties and the methods employed by the Comintern remained faithful in general to Lenin's doctrine in the circumstances that presented themselves. The role of the Comintern in the Spanish Civil War reflected the new tendency of the Kremlin to a greater degree than did the equivocal policy of the French Communist party after the victory of the Front Populaire in France in May, 1946. In Spain Comintern agents directed by André Marty had begun to carry out as their primary objective the new policy of liquidating deviationists and the strong Trotskyite movement in Catalonia. The elimination of opponents and the creation of a subservient tool took precedence over all other considerations.

However, in France the tactics pursued by the French Communist party after the left-wing victory in 1946 were in line with the classic Leninist policy of embracing your victim in order the better to destroy him. Thus the French Communists gave support to the Socialists in power in order to create such havoc as to be able to discredit and supplant them.

According to the doctrine developed during the second World War, the role of making the revolution was assigned to the Red Army. Communist parties outside the Soviet Union were to wait for the arrival of the Red Army. They were not to attempt a full-fledged revolution on their own. They were to act as auxiliaries to the Red Army.

This writer came upon direct evidence of this policy several weeks before D-Day. He was then stationed as a correspondent in Moscow. A friend brought him the manuscript of a radio broadcast which Maurice Thorez, the secretary general of the French Communist party, who was then living in Moscow, was to make over Radio Moscow to the Communist underground in France. The text ordered the French Communist underground to rise on D-Day and seize all the town halls and prefectures and arrest all who had collaborated with the Vichy regime or who were suspected of collaborating with the Germans. The series of specific instructions contained in Thorez' manuscript meant one, and only one, thing—armed insurrection and revolution on D-Day.

These orders were not carried out. The French Communists and left-wingers alleged after the liberation of France that the orders were never carried out because the Soviet Government did not wish to collide with the American and British Governments at the time or that the Anglo-American army would have crushed the insurrection. The readiness with which French Communists alleged these reasons in private was prima facie proof that they were only a dodge. When this writer put it to a French Comintern agent that the Soviet Government had in reality betrayed the French Communist party and the long-prepared French Communist revolution the agent turned away grimly.

It was the Yugoslav Communist party which put the finger on the official existence of such a doctrine in the Soviet Union. The Yugoslavs argued that the auxiliary role assigned to the non-Soviet Communist parties meant the death of the "international workers' movement" and the workers' revolution because in effect the Communist parties outside the Soviet Union were being told that hereafter they were only to act as aides to Soviet foreign policy and that there was to be no revolution in their countries without direct intervention by the Red Army. Yugoslav theorists maintain that the recession of the Communist parties of Western Europe is directly attributable to the satellite functions assigned to them by the Soviet leaders.

It would be purely academic to assume that the aggression in Korea does not bear the Soviet trade-mark or that such a thing as an independent North Korean Army exists. Too much is known about the origins, training, leadership and armament of the North Korean Army not to accept the fact that it is as much an instrument of Soviet policy as is the Far Eastern Soviet Army whose headquarters is at Kharbarovsk.

If in the weeks preceding the Normandy D-Day we saw the first implementation of the new Soviet policy in France, where the French Communist underground was ordered to desist from making the revolution, in North Korea we are witnessing the active principle of the policy whereby the Red Army, or a thinly disguised branch of the Red Army, tries to make the revolution.

In the Twenties and Thirties political thinkers were correct in assuming that the Soviet leaders would employ every means of aggrandizement short of war. The abandonment of the German Communist party in 1932 was adequate proof. However, there is one aspect of Soviet policy to which Western political observers should be accustomed by now, and that is its constant practical changes in order to achieve permanent objectives. The internal political structure of the Soviet dictatorship of today bears no more resemblance to the dictatorship of the proletariat exercised collectively by Lenin's Central Committee than does the Soviet military power of today resemble that of the pre-war era.

The Soviet's sphere of influence today encompasses continents as a result of the last war. Its army is the most powerful in the world and is in a permanent state of readiness. That does not mean that the Soviet leaders will be so crude as to commit their own home army in an adventure. There is no longer any need for that. The Soviet Army command has shown first-rate talents in creating non-Soviet armies and in transforming them into excellent fighting machines to do their bidding. The North Korean Army has been eloquent testimony to this policy.

The Soviet Army is now concentrating its attention on the armies of Poland, Czechoslovakia, Hungary, Rumania, Bulgaria, and Albania. While sterile debates have been going on in Western Europe on the question of rearmament, the Soviet Army command has already been able to raise more than one million fighting men in Eastern Europe, including ten or more armored divisions and many motorized divisions.

While the Governments of Western Europe continue to bicker about increasing the number of troops, the cost of rearmament, the question of who will be in command, and so on, the Soviet Army continues to increase daily the strength of its satellites' armies, two of which alone—the Polish and Czech armies—could march across Germany to Paris with only several American divisions to oppose them.

The aggression in Korea and the methods used by the Soviet leaders are handwriting on the wall for any Government of Western Europe which still has vision enough to be able to read. In two or three years' time the European satellite armies of the Soviet Union may be doubled. This instrument, skillfully employed by the Soviet command, will be able to do the job without committing a single division from the Soviet Union itself.

As time goes on, the satellite armies of the Soviet Union are bound to become a more and more important factor in the political orientation of Europe as a whole. They will play the role that the Soviet Army plays today in the European balance of power and leave the Soviet Army free to exert pressure elsewhere—possibly in the countries of the Middle East and India.

That is the future seen through Eastern European Marxists' eyes. One discordant element in this view has been the reaction in the United States to the aggression in Korea and the embarkation of the American Government on a rearmament program. The shrieks of the Stockholm "peace movement" only became more shrill at the spectacle of American rearmament because the Eastern European Marxists know full well that when American industry starts producing tanks and guns and planes they will pour out in floods. Any restraint which could be put on the American rearmament program would remove the only shadow cast on the vision of a rosy future which the Cominform Communists have.

Eastern European Marxists discount the Continental Western European countries. They regard them as sitting ducks. The only real obstacle to their plans—the obstacle which they fear to face— is a fully rearmed United States. It would be a mistake to believe that they fear a disarmed United States. Proof of this is in the aggression in Korea. The Soviet leaders are not concerned with potential power but with real power, and as long as the United States delays taking the necessary decisions to mobilize its industry and transform itself into an armed camp, more Soviet adventures can be expected.

The essential weakness of the American position has been that for too long the Government has permitted the Soviet Government to dictate its policies. The United States took a decision to withdraw from Korea several years ago on the grounds that the country was indefensible. Yet the Soviet leaders chose Korea as their first battlefield and propelled the Americans into it against their better judgment.

The Soviet Government can almost be said to have dictated the time for American rearmament. In Germany, the Russians play the tune in their Eastern zone and the Americans must dance accordingly in their Western zone. Almost every American action in Western Germany has been a reaction to Soviet initiative rather than a result of creative thinking and planning. The Marshall Plan in itself was born of necessities created by Soviet political action.

It is most unlikely that the new Soviet policy which has found its full expression for the first time in the Korean aggression will be scrapped, despite the national unity it has restored in the United States and the impetus it has given to the American rearmament program. The Soviet Government has already achieved the twofold objective of striking terror in the enfeebled Governments and social systems of Western Europe and of envenoming relations between Communist China and the United States to the point where a resumption of American political action in China has been postponed indefinitely.

The new Soviet policy cannot be regarded as anything but a direct reflection of the heights reached by the bureaucratic dictatorship in Moscow. In order to scrap its present policy and revert to the old Comintern method as an exclusive instrument it would be necessary for something approaching an internal revolution to take place in the Soviet Union. A return to the old Comintern concept of world revolution could not be brought about without restoration of the collective dictatorship of the Soviet Central Committee and the Leninist principle of collective responsibility and equality. It is only through a restoration of collective responsibility that the policy of imperial aggression and its present instrument—the policy of 1943-44—could be possibly scrapped.

This does not mean that the Soviet leaders are not prepared to use Comintern methods wherever they may be useful in order to further their imperialist designs. This would not be the first time that the Soviet leaders have preserved labels in order to destroy both content and intent of their announced policies.

How the President Makes Decisions

by Anthony Leviero

NO PRESIDENT in history has had to make more decisions of great moment than Harry S. Truman. From the determination to use the A-bomb against Japan to the order to defend South Korea, his judgments have literally shaped history. How does Mr. Truman arrive at the great conclusions he has to reach?

Mr. Truman's decisions represent the sum of three influences—the researches and recommendations of his advisers, his own pragmatic experience and his willingness in moments of crisis to give heed to his own deep hunches.

On occasion Mr. Truman has been guilty of making "snap judgments." This was particularly true in those early months when he was new to the power of the Presidency. But he has learned his lesson from those unhappy experiences and now depends in most cases upon his team of advisers and consultants. He uses these aides like so many extra pairs of eyes and ears to stoke his mind with the facts of a situation before rendering a judgment. When a problem arises, he relies on the thoroughness of the analyses and digests placed before him. The weighing process that goes on in his mind produces few visible symptoms. He makes his decisions forthrightly, and it is evident that they are made in good conscience.

As much as a half to two-thirds of his time is spent studying the reports of his assistants and listening to their arguments preparatory to making the multitudinous decisions which are required of him. But though he may put infinite reliance in the information they furnish him and the judgments they make, the ultimate decision will be labeled "Truman." He cannot pin responsibility on any member of his official family nor avoid the consequences of their errors and shortcomings. He does not hesitate to dismiss them if they fail him, however.

There seems to be little doubt that the top of the hierarchy is occupied by the man who most recently became a member, General Marshall, the Secretary of Defense. He was called back from retirement at the age of 69 to quench the fires of hostility and distrust, both within the Cabinet and among a large segment of the public, that had raged around the incumbency of Louis Johnson. That the General will accomplish this seems almost a foregone conclusion. There are few men in the nation more heavily weighted with honors or whose careers have been marked by more selfless devotion to duty.

Sharing the leadership is Secretary of State Acheson who will suffer no loss of position or prestige as a result of the recent Cabinet shift. That he has had the President's full confidence is widely known, and it was powerfully underscored when the President, at long last, resolved the friction between him and Secretary Johnson by allowing the latter to resign.

W. Averell Harriman is described by some observers as the Harry Hopkins of the Truman Administration, but the term is not too accurate. Apart from other considerations, there has not been time enough for such a relationship as existed between Roosevelt and Hopkins to develop between Truman and Harriman. Yet it is quite apparent that Mr. Truman is using Harriman on a much broader basis than is implied by his title of Special Assistant to the President on foreign policy. He helps to integrate domestic and foreign policy at many points where they overlap. His experience with the Western European allies and as Ambassador to Moscow and Secretary of Commerce is now paying off.

Mr. Harriman's recent mission to impress on General MacArthur this country's grave concern with Far Eastern policy—a policy centered at Lake Success and not Tokyo—was one of high trust, in the category of a Hopkins mission to Stalin. The President also relied on Mr. Harriman's advice in defining the scope of controls that would be necessary in a partial mobilization, and in revamping the staff of the National Security Council.

Mr. Truman has a steady and respected adviser on military details in that calm fellow Missourian, Gen. Omar N. Bradley. The man who looks like a schoolmaster but is acknowledged as the foremost of the strategists we produced in World War II has won the utmost confidence of the Commander in Chief. In a practical sense General Bradley fills the job of Chief of Staff to the President that Mr. Truman abolished with the retirement of Fleet Admiral William D. Leahy last year. During the Korean War, he has gone to the Oval Room in the White House each morning at 9:30 to brief the President on the war situation and to discuss larger problems of strategy and military policy.

W. Stuart Symington acts as the channel through which the President is kept informed of the progress and the needs of the mobilization program—his official position being that of chairman of the National Security Resources Board. He has been delegated most of the special powers over industry, manpower, raw materials and prices which were vested in the President by the War Production Act.

John R. Steelman, who bears the unique title, The Assistant to the President, is a top coordinator on the administrative level. He bridges the gap between the President and a multitude of responsibilities arising from all over the sprawling Federal bureaucracy.

Charles S. Murphy, special counsel to the President, operates at the same level as an adviser on policy-making. Both these officials are in daily communication with the President, at regular morning staff meetings and at odd times throughout the day as well. They carry a large share of the President's personal burden.

These are the men and the policy-making machinery that assist the President to make up his mind. In considering the President's leadership role it should be emphasized that in making decisions affecting grave issues of national security Mr. Truman relies on collective recommendations presented in council rather than on the advice of individual advocates. He works by a firm rule that his team must get together, thrash out problems and resolve differences before they come to him for decision. He does not mind settling differences himself if his advisers cannot agree, but first he must be satisfied that they have tried their darndest.

That was the procedure, for example, that preceded the decision to intervene in Korea. The effect of this rule of policy-making in council has been to subordinate, perhaps more than at any time in our history, the influence of individual advisers and increase the weight of the judgment of group deliberations in agencies such as the National Security Council, the Joint Chiefs of Staff and the National Security Resources Board.

Members of the Cabinet are required to serve as members of the council and the board, so that they constitute an interlocking directorate that is designed to integrate all phases of domestic, foreign and military policy-making. It can be argued with some justification that these agencies have failed to meet the test of national security and that in large measure they can be only as good as the men that constitute them. Certainly the council, with its accessory Central Intelligence Agency, and the Joint Chiefs of Staff are no guarantees against Pearl Harbors, as the new day of infamy in Korea demonstrated.

Mr. Truman has sought to increase the effectiveness of these agencies by tightening up their inter-relationships and supervising them more closely. He has directed Mr. Harriman to attend meetings of the Cabinet, the N. S. C. and the N. S. R. B. Similarly, Mr. Symington attends meetings of the Cabinet and N. S. C., while Dr. Steelman sits in with N. S. R. B.

Given this system of planning and deliberation, how then does Mr. Truman come to grips with big issues when the chips are down? For the answer one has to scrutinize the fabric of his character and his stewardship as Chief Executive in five years of continual crisis.

By those who have worked with him for years, Mr. Truman is pictured as a man of courage. In making decisions tough beyond words he is upset neither by toughness nor the disagreements of reasonable men. He realizes that problems would not come to him unless they were tough to begin with.

Mr. Truman is a pragmatist—he believes in methods that work. In view of a lingering tendency to belittle Mr. Truman as a politician favored by luck, it is something of a revelation to hear members of his staff and of his Cabinet describe him as an excellent administrator. This is not a capacity that is found plentifully among politicians or lawyers. Mr. Truman recognizes good staff work when it exists, and is uncomfortable when it is faulty. If he feels a disputed issue has been thrashed out, he will take over and settle it promptly. Otherwise he will tell those concerned to come in with more facts.

The Chief Executive insists that all his decisions are to be reduced to writing. A Cabinet officer who has worked with other Presidents regards this as one of his finest practices. He recalls how the oral instructions of some of Mr. Truman's predecessors were interpreted according to the particular predilections of those who heard them, causing confusion and recriminations.

Mr. Truman's system is this: He has recommendations in writing. If he approves a recommendation, he signs it and it becomes policy. If there is a divergence of opinion he will say, "I approve the one I am now signing." Or if he makes a change, he writes it on the document over his signature. Thus his decisions are in black and white and not easily misconstrued.

"He doesn't fuss you," said one of his official family. "After he gives you a decision he leaves it to you to implement it."

Reports, digests, summaries and memoranda flow to the President's desk by the score each day. The bulk of his study of this mass of documents is reserved for the afternoons. Most evenings he fills a brown leather brief case with those he has not gone through during the day and takes them to the quiet of Blair House with him. He is, fortunately, a rapid and a retentive reader. If a question arises he may pick up the telephone and call one of his aides for clarification. Or, if he is at Blair House, he will scribble a note as a reminder for the next morning.

Frequently a report comes to him reflecting the unresolved differences in viewpoint of several people. In such cases, he may call the contestants in and explore their differences in a desk-side conference. When he has heard them out, and if it seems that the problem will not yield to yet further study, he is most likely to make a decision on the spot.

Mr. Truman's approach to problems is practical. His mind does not soar on wings of imagination. He contemplates a proposition in terms of the here and now; its concreteness and desirability. He never loses sight of the thorny path that lies between desire and possession.

Hunches, however, play a part in his decisions. That may stem from his belief in his rightness, from his ingrained self-confidence. It is also probable that, consciously or otherwise, he shares the widespread impression about himself that he is "just an average man" and that his tastes, aspirations and reactions are those of a majority of the American people. Thus, when he weighs a problem in statecraft, some of that intangible element, intuition, goes into the scales along with the facts, the figures and the cold logic.

How is the President bearing up under the strains of the crisis? In the first weeks of the Korean war he was tense and profoundly disturbed. His concern, apart from the tough decision to commit American troops in a desperate fight, was that his greatest hope —to be the world's foremost leader in working for a real and lasting peace—might be blasted. He did not smile as often as he formerly did, and one was impressed with the hard set of his jaw.

In spite of all the delegated work of his team system, Mr. Truman comes ultimately to the period when he must wrestle with problems himself and in solitude. A general arriving at Blair House one Sunday afternoon seeking a signature on an important document found the President alone in his study burrowing into a big stack of papers and reports. It is in such hours that the President works out his own doubts. He does no soul-searching in public, and that is one of the qualities that win support for his leadership.

In the Long Run Europe
Is Our First Front

by Nathaniel Peffer

IF WASHINGTON, Jefferson, Hamilton, Franklin and others of the Founding Fathers of the Republic were to revisit the earth to survey the progress of what they had wrought, they would no doubt be startled by skyscrapers, airplanes, telephone and radio. But what would puzzle them most would be what on earth had brought it about that the republic they had founded along a narrow fringe of the Atlantic seaboard should, in seven generations, have come to pledge its life, its fortunes and its honor on the concerns of the continent on the other side of the Pacific.

If it were on the concerns of Europe, they might regret it, believing, as they did, that the Union's safety lay in detachment from external politics, but they would understand, since they regarded themselves as Englishmen and therefore Europeans. But why Asia? That they could not understand.

It is a question that must sometimes puzzle contemporary Americans, too. For one of the main preoccupations of this country in this generation has been the politics of the Far East, and it was act ally because of the Japanese invasion of China and not because of the Nazis' conquest of nearly all Europe that America was brought into the last war. Still more, America has been torn within for a decade, part of it looking westward to Asia, part of it looking eastward to Europe—very much like Russia since the eighteenth century.

This was most dramatically in evidence after Pearl Harbor, when there was a sharp controversy, not always in the open, over the strategy of the war, the issue being whether to concentrate first on Germany or first on Japan. Owing to the firmness of President Roosevelt and General Marshall, the decision was in favor of defeating Germany first, but there was bitterness both within the fighting services and without.

Now there is a "cold war," and the controversy has been revived. Again the issue is: shall this country concentrate its efforts on Asia or on Europe? Russia threatens in both. Where shall we try to check it first? There is an immediate contingency, and as long as the Chinese and North Koreans, or both, are threatening, America has no choice and cannot withdraw. But, in the long run, broader considerations enter and, for the long-run, decisions should be made on those considerations.

Now, however, the issue is political as well as military, and therefore more productive of rancor. It is political both externally and internally; externally, in that, by diplomatic pressure, economic measures and the establishment of strong points we are engaged in almost every part of the world; internally, in that the most acrid controversy in domestic politics now turns on what the present Administration in Washington has or has not done in the Far East.

One thing has to be said. The controversy now raging is not always waged on the merits of the issue. It is clear that a great deal of the partisanship of all-out efforts for Asia is a disguised or oblique isolationism. Many of those who would let France go to save Formosa do not care so much about either as they do about letting the rest of the world "stew in its own juice." The solicitude for Chiang Kai-shek and Bao Dai can be a symbolic expression of resentment of the "aberration" of Woodrow Wilson, Franklin Roosevelt and influential leaders in the Atlantic seaboard. It is, in many cases, sometimes unconsciously, sometimes sincerely, a rationale for regression.

How has it come about? Why the preoccupation with Asia and how far is it justified? The question is not new, even if never before so urgent as now. It has been mounting toward fixity since the beginning of this century and principally it concerns China. It arises out of what has become an increasingly firm resolve to permit no great power to have control over that country.

In the first years of the century, the opposition was directed against Russia, which, then as now, had outposts in Manchuria and was manifesting aspirations to expand from there down into China proper. There were sharp diplomatic brushes between Washington and St. Petersburg, though with more decorum in vocabulary than can be found at Lake Success now.

This ended when Japan disposed of Russia in the war of 1904-1905 and was succeeded by the same situation between the United States and Japan over the same places and for the same reasons. Japan had supplanted Russia in Manchuria and was manifesting the same unmistakable desire to take all of China. This ended only with the ceremonies on the U. S. S. Missouri on Sept. 2, 1945.

Among students of American foreign policy, there has never been agreement on why America has staked so much on the preservation of China's independence; outwardly, so much more than it has on the fate of any single European country. The reasons are mixed, as in all politics, but, originally, the main reason appears to have been more economic than anything else.

It is true that trade with China constituted a negligible fraction of American foreign trade, but the lure of what would come when China would be fully opened to foreign commerce and fully developed has exercised a fascination for almost a hundred years. This has changed now. The chief consideration is no longer economic but strategic. It has to do with American security. The hope of gain has given way to fear—fear of the danger that would be created by a Russia extending from Berlin to the Pacific. To that

"economic threat?"

must be added ideological fear—fear of an all-powerful Russia that is also Communist.

Russia in Asia is even more difficult to explain. All the conventional motivations of foreign policy do not seem to fit except as an explanation after the fact. Clearly, the motive cannot be economic, since Russia is still relatively unindustrialized, under-populated and rich in resources. It cannot be the need for security, since Russia proper never has been menaced by the weak nations and tribes of Asia. There is, rather, something elemental in Russia's eastward expansion, something geological, something glacial, moving slowly but relentlessly. At any rate, Russia was moving eastward across Asia as early as three hundred years ago. By the middle of the nineteenth century it was in full course, and before the end of the century had arrived at the shores of the Pacific. Now, it appears to be solidly entrenched and still advancing. But even now it is impossible to say with assurance whether it moves as an empire in the classical sense, in a way Peter the Great would have approved, or as the vehicle of social revolution carrying Marxism to the Eastern World. Whatever the motives may be on both sides, the position is clear. Russia expands in Asia and America seeks to stop it. At the same time, Russia expands in Europe and America (as well as Western Europe) seeks to stop it there, too. But where shall America direct its major effort—to Europe or to Asia? As in 1942, it has not enough power to attempt both simultaneously without being ineffective in both. Which shall it subordinate?

There is only one logical approach to the question. If the ultimate choice were forced in the immediate future by acts or events beyond our control, which of the two could be lost without jeopardizing America's continued existence as a nation? Could we survive more easily, or, at least, be in less danger, if all Europe fell to Russia, or if all Asia fell to Russia?

Suppose, for example, Asia were lost. Just what would be the consequences to America? Economically, it would be unfortunate, but in future potentiality rather than present reality. It would restrict future opportunity, but not inflict at once a penalty that would be reflected in the American economy. At the worst, not all trade would cease. There was trade with Soviet Russia even before American recognition in 1933. The economic loss, in other words, would be relative rather than absolute.

Strategically, the consequences would be much more serious. Europe would become politically, as well as geographically, a peninsula. The whole Eurasian land mass, with the exception of India and Pakistan at least for a time, would be at Russia's disposal, for political, economic and military purposes. There would be created the largest political unit the world has known. But would it be for a long time the most formidable in terms of actual threat to highly organized and technically efficient societies such as those of Western Europe and North America?

Let it be assumed that the whole of China's power is Russia's to use—an assumption not yet warranted in the long run. China has numbers, no doubt. It could provide an army of tens of millions. But as yet Chinese troops have been trained for old-fashioned, small-arms warfare and guerrilla resistance only. They were effective against the demoralized, incompetently led armies of Chiang Kai-shek and for slow attrition of small Japanese units, but they would be of doubtful use against a modern army unless superiority of numbers were so overwhelming as to smother it by sheer mass. The North Koreans, it must be remembered, were dispersed in three weeks, despite their Russian tanks, when the American forces arrived in comparable numbers.

Aside from manpower, the accession of China, even if it were without reservation, would add little to Russian strength in the near future. China is yet without any real industry. It cannot make a tank or a heavy gun or even a jeep, let alone jet planes. It has only the most rudimentary beginning of industrialization and cannot accelerate the process very much, since it lacks both capital and technical personnel. It will be all the Communist regime can do to keep the country's head above water without a forced pace in industrialization. Even if Russia had the capacity to industrialize China and thus provide it with powerful armament, which is doubtful in any period short of decades, there is no assurance that it would do so. Why should it want a really powerful country on its outermost boundaries, next to some of its most important new industrial centers? What guarantee has it that a strong China would always be at its disposal or even friendly? Despite the presumed ideological affinity, there is no reason to assume that Russia has an excessive trust in China or vice versa, most of all vice versa.

Suppose, too, that Russia were entrenched on the Pacific shore of Asia by virtue of controlling China. How much difference would that make? It is on the Pacific shore of Asia now at Vladivostok, which is closer to San Francisco or Detroit than Shanghai. It is still closer at Kamchatka, opposite the Aleutian Islands, from which it could attack American cities much more easily than from China bases.

All this is to say that Russian possession of all Asia would be serious but not fatal, at least for a long time, long enough for Europe to be strengthened and its military and economic potential to be integrated with America's.

But if Europe were lost to Russia? Then there would be economic consequences indeed. A large and important segment of America's export trade would be cut off—automobiles, farm machinery, business machines, machine tools, grains, meat, tobacco and cotton. All would remain to glut the home market. Further, the billions lent to European countries during the war and afterward through E. C. A. would have to be written off. America, no doubt, could make the required adjustments, but the blow would be a crippling one.

More grave would be the strategic consequences. For then, Russia would have the whole world, except America, which would stand as an island in a vast militarist-Communist sea. Asia could go Communist and Europe remain unaffected, but if Europe became Communist, Asia would fall into line almost automatically. It would see the handwriting on the wall. Certainly, no part of it would have enough confidence in America to risk aligning itself with the United States.

Physically, America would be under direct threat. Russia would have at its disposal not only European manpower but Europe's industrial establishment and its advanced technological development, both in plant and personnel. This last might be the greatest lift to Russia from European conquest. Moreover, it would have convenient and easy jumping-off places for attack on America.

Ireland, the United Kingdom, the Iberian Peninsula, Greenland, Iceland, the Azores, North Africa and Dakar—all are springboards. Then America would really be surrounded. It would have to become an armed camp, standing unremittingly on guard, all other considerations in American society—education, health, welfare—subordinated to the military. That alone would constitute defeat, would negate the promise of American destiny.

There is something else, more intangible, but no less compelling. The prospect of all Western Europe coming under the brutish, atavistic regimen of Russian monolithic totalitarianism is not easily tolerable. Everything slowly grown and formed since the Renaissance, since the Dark Ages even, would be nullified. Western culture would be truncated. The West, after all, has developed slowly, in traditions and institutions of representative, responsible government and guarantees of equality under the law administered in channels of justice openly conducted.

It is not pleasant to think of Scandinavians, Hollanders, Frenchmen and Englishmen going to bed at night wondering whether the 2 A. M. knock on the door will come and, if it comes, being dragged off and dropped somewhere into oblivion, their wives and children never knowing where they were or whether they were dead or alive, their kindest fate that of being hauled off to some Arctic slave camp. It is not pleasant to think of a Churchill confessing before the microphone at a trial after being held incommunicado for months; or an Attlee or a Herriot or a Bertrand Russell or an André Gide—confessing to anything and everything and then being dragged off to be shot as even common criminals are no longer shot.

It is not pleasant to think of a British physicist or a French philosopher standing up at a public hearing, renouncing all his previous beliefs in the light of the pronouncements of Great Stalin, Father and Protector of England and France, light of the world, inventor of fire and the wheel, architect of the Parthenon, author of "Hamlet," painter of the Sistine Chapel, composer of the Ninth Symphony, discoverer of electricity. It is not pleasant to think of all Europeans cowering in terror all their living moments, forever turning their heads to see who was listening, fearful always of the informer, not knowing whether their own children would report on them.

Then, surely, night would settle on Europe and there would be an end of all that has given Western civilization its dignity.

Consciously to elect this in order to save Formosa and Indo-China and Burma—that requires a resoluteness not easily come by, except as the last, the uttermost price of survival. And that it is not. On any fair examination of the issue on its merits we are not yet at that point. We can save ourselves and the world if we hold Europe, though we lose Asia. We can lose the world and ourselves if we lose Europe, though we hold Asia.

It is much as it was in 1942. We cannot come fully to the defense of both continents. A choice as to priority must be made in order to be successful in both in the end. Now as then the claim of Europe is greater. We shall stand or fall in Europe.

Tense Lands in China's Shadow

by Hanson W. Baldwin

IN THE KOREAN mountains the dull weight of winter already was pressing down upon the land . . . The rain fell in slow insistence in Tokyo . . . Thirteen hundred miles to the south, above Formosa Strait, the wind-torn cloud-rack, whipped by a forty-mile monsoon, rocked and buffeted the plane . . . Around "The Peak" in Hong Kong the mist lay draped; Repulse Bay, ancient haunt of pirates and smugglers, was veiled with grayness . . . And in Saigon, one-time "Paris of the East," the damp heat oppressed and irritated and seemed to warn of distant disaster.

Throughout the Orient the weather provided a fitting backdrop for the political climate. From Kyushu to Taiwan, from Hanoi to Seoul, there was tension and the overbearing and ominous foreboding of events. Throughout the Orient there was war, or the talk of war; the gauntlet has been thrown down in Asia and thousands of men from scores of different races march and shoot and die—from the sub-Arctic cold of Korea to the sticky tropical heat of Indo-China's river deltas.

From the *New York Times Magazine,* December 24, 1950, copyright © 1950 by The New York Times Company.

To the traveler along what the geopoliticians call Asia's strategic "rimlands"—Korea, Japan, Formosa, Hong Kong, French Indo-China—there are in addition to this sense of foreboding, this atmosphere of impending storm which seems to hang over Asia, two other common denominators which link these scattered lands in a common pattern.

One is the fecund, teeming millions of the Orient; wherever one goes there is febrile life, often scabrous, dirty, diseased, but thronging and persistent. Like animals, many of the masses of Asia live and breed and die; like animals they persist, fatalistic, determined, undeterred—driven by the great primitive instincts to eat, to breed, to acquire.

The other factor common to all the Asian littoral—a factor now that casts a long shadow across our world—is Red China. This is the sullen enigma—the brooding, ominous giant—that looms over the rimlands; this is the mysterious, almost primeval, force which now shapes the destiny of the Orient.

Stalin was once supposed to have asked sardonically and contemptuously: "How many divisions has the Pope?" Throughout Asia the divisions that Red China can put into the field provide the common denominator that links the fortunes of Korea with those of Japan, Formosa, Hong Kong and Indo-China.

Korea

From the air the land looks peaceful until one sees the bomb-bay doors open and a salvo of 500-pounders wobble downward to strike in smoke puffs and flame bursts of destruction. The bursting bombs punctuate the rugged landscape, but bombing—even at optimum altitude of 12,000 to 14,000 feet as our B-29's do it in Korea—is an impersonal, abstract form of patterned violence; you see only the awesome effects, none of the blood and sweat and tears.

Korea presents a curious cartography to the bombardier's eye—a tangled, twisted mass of rugged mountains, stubbled with small timber, snow-capped in the north, laced with many streams and rivers—ice-locked now—and in the valleys and up the terraces of the hills the fantastic patterns of the rice paddies, green and golden and yellow, broken now and again by wasteland, red as the clay of Georgia, corrugated like the mountains of the moon.

But on the ground the beauty fades; the injustice and indiscriminate horrors of war become personalized. The road from Inchon to the airfield at Kimpo and across the turgid Han to Seoul is a road where armies have marched and fought; upon the map this area may some day be marked with the crossed swords of the geographer, but now it has more viable meaning to the homeless, the crippled and the slain.

The waterfront at Inchon is a monument to the destructiveness of high explosive; warehouse walls topple dangerously; burnt-out skeletons of buildings stare with empty eyes toward the Yellow Sea; up the hill in the ruins of Inchon's slums the poor are scrabbling in the shards and dust for their few but precious belongings; with painful effort they build new "homes"—tiny shelters of mats and rice straw.

On the road to Kimpo the tide of battle is plainly marked; here a village is intact and the children swarm; the Korean elder with his conical hat and long pipe basks in the sun; war has passed them by. A half mile farther on the enemy stood—and died—and with him died the cluster of thatched-roof houses he tried to defend—nothing now but burned-black heaps of rice straw, soggy with rain, offensive to the nose . . . There are burned-out tanks and over-turned trucks along the roads of Korea, and there are, too, the human flotsam and jetsam of conflict. On a hillside, facing toward the warm south, lie the graves beneath the U. N. flag—the marines and doughboys who paid the price of capturing Seoul. And on this and every road there are the living whom war has dispossessed—the refugees, eternally going or coming, their most precious possessions piled on bicycles, dumped on trucks, carried in carts behind their oxen.

Seoul—at the best of times a city of drabness and poverty—is half destroyed; great gaps where buildings used to be, and always the odor of water-soaked, fire-blackened rice straw and other smells more pungent and sickening.

Throughout Korea the same impersonal destructiveness of war has blasted bridges, filled streets with rubble, reduced freight yards and factories to twisted steel and water-filled craters. Yet clustered round the wreckage, poking through the debris, moving endlessly down the streets and roads, toiling from dawn to dusk in the rice paddies, the women pausing briefly to nurse their babies by the wayside, hauling incredible burdens on the A-frames on their back, are the persistent, patient peasants, hundreds of them, thousands of them, millions of them—the peoples of Asia engaged eternally in their struggle to live.

There is always a curious contrast in war behind the front and rear areas, but the war we have been fighting in Korea has been like no other. Never before have our pilots "commuted" from their homes to battle; never before has the contrast between the hardships of the front and the almost feverish gaiety of the rear seemed so accentuated.

Tokyo

Tokyo is a city of glaring contrasts; we, the conquerors, live high, wide and handsome; parties, dinners, dances and flirtations provide a silver screen obscuring but never completely hiding the grim background of Korea. There is sometimes almost a frenetic gaiety; worried wives try to find in social functions release and escape— not alone from the worry of war, but from the boredom of idleness. The silver gleams; the cocktails are good; the wines are vintages; the liquers are numerous and the uniforms shine in the candlelight; at the door, the kimono-clad servants lined up in a row bow profoundly to the departing guests.

But in the Dai Ichi building, headquarters of SCAP (Supreme Commander, Allied Powers) the lights shine far into the night and are reflected in the turgid waters of the moat surrounding the Imperial Palace.

At a Japanese dinner, as a geisha fills the little cups with sake, a Japanese newspaper man says:

"A retired general told me we would need a minimum of eighteen divisions—several of them armored—to defend Japan."

Formosa

The Generalissimo in his plain khaki uniform with no badge of rank, no row of ribbons, gestures with his eloquent, graceful hands; he states his case and pleads his cause with the fervor of the young. To see him you would think that this man—his life so closely entwined with the history of China for the past thirty years—was a benevolent schoolmaster rather than a politician. There are laughter wrinkles at the eyes; he bows politely, smiles easily, says, "How, how," and, "Ah, ah"; only now and again as he becomes impassioned do you see in the dark depths of the eyes the hardness, even the ruthlessness, that any man must possess who would be a power in Chinese politics.

The "G-mo" and Madame Chiang sit on rose-brocaded furniture in front of embroidered tapestries, rich in color, modest in their Oriental splendor. Their home is guarded closely, and the Nationalist Government and the Nationalist Army are infiltrated with a political commissar system (headed by Chiang Kai-shek's older son) which is calculated to discourage all would-be Communists or usurpers.

For even Formosa, separated by one hundred miles of windswept strait from the mainland, lies beneath the shadow of the Red colossus; indeed, the lives of many of its people are conditioned reflexes to communism.

At a twelve-course Chinese dinner—including rice wine, 1,000-year-old eggs and sea slugs—a Chinese colonel proposes a toast. "To victory," he says. "A united China."

On Formosa—as throughout the Orient—the atmosphere is martial; the heavy hand of war counts the progress of the hours. In the gray dawn, while sleepers toss beneath their mosquito netting, Chinese buglers practice battle calls in discordant cacophony. Incongruously the military bands play the Chinese favorites—"Red Wings," "Lady of Spain," "Stars and Stripes Forever," and—for funerals—"Dixie."

In the south, around Kao Hsiung, where many of the training

activities of the Nationalist Army, Navy and Air Force are located, the military atmosphere is even more evident. The police in military uniforms check travelers' papers at every station. In the camps where General Sun Li-Jen, commander of the army ground forces, has set up Chinese replicas of our Fort Benning and of our officer candidate schools, Chinese soldiers—often stripped to the waist, with conical straw hats, straw sandals or rubber sneakers—engage en masse in the physical toughening exercises that form so large a part of all Chinese Army training. Tugs of war, log exercises, butts manual, obstacle courses, and bayonet drill with the participants chanting in Chinese, "Kill! kill!," are part of the course.

At mess and on the ranges, the austerity to which the Nationalists have been reduced is noticeable. The ration is somewhat meager—bowls of rice with bean cake gravy, bits of fat pork and green vegetables, the latter culled from the soldiers' gardens, tilled carefully each afternoon to supplement their diet. Ammunition is used sparingly; there's none too much of it on Formosa if invasion comes.

Crowded on this island, upon which so many different cultures have been imposed by so many different conquerors, is the largest anti-Communist army in the Orient—of doubtful quality, true; deficient in equipment, true; uncertain in morale, true—but nevertheless the biggest integrated anti-Communist force in being.

Hong Kong

The city where East meets West and both make profits, magnificent in its dignified beauty, roiled by all the political turmoils of the Orient, filled with the alarums of war, is nevertheless perhaps most acutely conscious of stock market quotations, currency exchange rates and commodity prices. The "Hong Kong Hymn," authored by a newspaper man long in the Orient, epitomizes and satirizes the conflicting motives—commercial and military—that dominate life in the crown colony:

In Hong Kong it's clear
The Man of the Year
   Must either be Stalin or Mao.
We call out the Tommies
To keep out the commies
   But take in their shekels
   —And HOW!
The world's in a mess
But commercial success
Is ours, so we couldn't
   care less.
But we're telling you
That we've consciences, too
   That we take from the safe
   once a week.
It's a business man's bet
That the Lord won't
   forget
   What he promised to do for
   the meek.

Up the winding narrow roads to "The Peak," and in the terraced highlands where rich Chinese refugees and long-time British Hong Kong residents live in new apartment houses and enjoy one of the world's most beautiful views, the stark skeletons of looted and destroyed buildings are acute reminders of a war still unfinished . . . Out at the Line in the Free Territories, where the thin red line of British Empire abuts upon the territory of Red China, British and British-trained Chinese police face Chinese Communist soldiers and customs officials across two bridges. Back and forth throughout the daylight hours, the flow of humanity is unceasing—Chinese peasants, laden with straw baskets move into China; Chinese peasants, laden with straw baskets, move into the Free Territories. The legal traffic in goods is considerable—trucks, penicillin, tires; the illegal, by smugglers' ruses, by black-market transactions, by pirates and bandits, by transshipment to junks in some of the hundreds of bays and waterways that surround Hong Kong and Kowloon, probably far exceeds the legal. Until recently Hong Kong and Macao were the principal gateways to the world of Communist China; through these treaty ports have poured the stuff Peiping has needed; now Thailand, one of the Orient's most prosperous nations, is probably the principal middleman between Communist China and the merchants of the earth.

The British profess confidence in their ability to defend Hong Kong in case of attack, but few objective observers believe the colony could withstand determined assault. A new system of land fortification has been built well back of the Line in the hills, but Hong Kong has some 300 miles of land frontier with China, and the defenders are few; the potential attackers—both within and without the colony—enormous.

But life goes on, as if on the lip of a volcano; the rickshaws and the sampans cluster and the coolies scream for patronage; the junks sail in and out past Stonecutters' Island; the sun sets past Repulse Bay and in, around and about Hong Kong, brightest diadem in the King's crown of empire, is the shouldering, swarming life of the Orient.

Saigon

At the Grand Hotel in Saigon even sheets are onerous to the touch; the damp heat settles like an oppressive blanket over the town . . . Beneath the shuttered windows of your room the streets pulsate with traffic—French colonial officers in shorts and open-necked shirts; paratroopers in berets, Senegalese, pretty Annamite women clad in their graceful silken *cai ao* and *cai quan* riding bicycles; passengers in *pousse-cycles,* or pedicabs (which have largely replaced the rickshaw in much of the Orient); an occasional car, or cab or truck. The Orient is still in the bicycle age—thousands swarm Saigon's streets.

But this sense of seeming peacefulness is illusory. Just a few months ago the Grand Hotel's sidewalk cafe—so well patronized now by French and foreigners having their before-dinner apéritifs

—was ugly with blood and bodies after some of the Vietminh Communist underground had tossed grenades among the crowded tables. Each French family in Saigon has an arsenal of its own; at night the residences of many of our diplomatic officials and of all leading French officials are surrounded by armed guards; if you go to see the High Commissioner, you dismount from the taxi outside the gate of his residence; the taxi might conceal a bomb . . .

Indo-China is torn day and night with the horrible realities of civil war; the French live beleaguered and sequestered lives—pleasant enough in the cities, always dangerous in the country; they have developed a crust of stoic fatalism; sufficient unto the day the evils thereof.

On the roads around Saigon—and around the Red River delta cities of Hanoi and Haiphong in the north near China—are innumerable towers, posts and forts, each with its little garrison, its tri-color or banner of the French-sponsored native state of Vietnam, its few pitiful guns. The towers—of wood, or brick, or concrete block, surrounded by a few rude shelters for the troops and *chevaux de fris* of sharpened bamboo stakes—dot the main roads about a kilometer apart; the posts—larger and more elaborate, but essentially of the same construction—are further apart: the forts, often manned by several companies or a battalion, are at the most important strategic locations. Despite these elaborate static defenses, supplemented by mobile patrols, the French rarely leave the cities without an escort of armed men; trucks and cars travel in convoys, and at night time the French retire into their stockades and leave the country to the Communist guerrilla . . .

Near Tanan, forty kilometers from Saigon, in the heart of a swamp and rice-paddy region, seamed by great sluggish muddy rivers, the little towers, bearing the emblem of French authority, seem rising from a sea of mud.

At the Hoa Phu post, commanded by a French sergeant, the garrison of twenty-seven men—three of them Europeans, the rest of them Vietnamese natives—stared out over a flat rain-lashed wilderness of rice paddies and delta lowlands, broken only occasionally by native huts and clumps of trees. The sergeant—short, stocky, tough—lived with the two other Frenchmen in a rectangular room of the tower, furnished only with cots with mosquito netting, a couple of chairs, a table, a gun rack. Above the room, on the top platform of the three-story tower was the sentry behind his loopholed parapet; tucked away in the roof above was a native shrine to keep away the spirits of bad luck.

The sergeant's life was the post of Hoa Phu; he had served there for twenty-two months; only once had he been to Saigon only forty kilometers away; never once had he spent the night in the town of Tanan, headquarters of his sector.

"What do you do?"

The sergeant shrugged, spreading his hands in that typical Gallic gesture which indicates a cheerful laissez-faire acceptance of fate:

"Non, we do not play cards; there are only three of us, besides, one does not play. We read, write letters home—yes, all of us are married, our families are in France—and we go on patrols . . ."

The sergeant's face lit up; he liked to go out hunting—manhunting, hunting for Ho Chi Minh's Communist-led Vietminh guerrillas . . .

At a sector headquarters not far away the French commandant and his officers preserve all the amenities traditional to the French Army—the apéritifs before dinner, the hors d'oeuvre, the many-course dinner, deliciously cooked, well-served, the wine, the champagne, the brandy—and the conversation, about France, the country, women—never about the war or the things of war . . .

"Bon appétit," says the junior member of the mess as the officers are seated. He reads the menu and then in flowing French—smiling—he recites the traditional speech repeated at every mess before each dinner:

"Bon appétit, messieurs, and may you all die with the last mouthful, beginning with the senior officer, in order to facilitate promotion in the French Army, by which, I (as the junior officer) will certainly be the last to profit."

The good conversation and good food, the ease of living with war seemingly far away, present an incongruous contrast to the coconut log barricade and earthworks outside, and to the ugly-looking sharpened bamboo stakes on which a man might become impaled so easily . . .

Later, on the way back to Saigon, its pretty Annamites and its pulsing life, the colonel turns, and comments in the same terms of fatalistic resignation one hears so often:

"It was a good country, a beautiful country, this—but now—fini."

As one flies home from the Orient, and the discordant, jumbled impressions that quick travel by air traces across the mind, a common pattern of tension seems to dominate all the countries along Asia's east coast.

Here in these "rimlands" is life—intense, feverish life, triumphant against great odds—but life so occupied with the struggle to continue and the struggle for power (which are perhaps synonymous in the Orient) that war, as someone has remarked, represents merely a difference in tension. Here in these coastal regions are peoples with few common interests save the desire for life, not yet subjects of Communist Governments, not yet cut off from the West, but most of them preoccupied with their own primitive needs, resentful of the West, groping, confused, stirring—peoples emerging (but barely) from feudalistic societies, peoples going they know not where.

Saigon: New Focus of Tension in Asia

by Peggy Durdin

SAIGON.

NERVE CENTER of a ruthless war between the Vietminh and the French, Vietnam's capital wears a prosperous, bustling facade which serves as a thin disguise for danger and insecurity.

French soldiers and sailors sit sipping leisured apéritifs in a sidewalk cafe on Saigon's main street, Rue Catinat. . . . In a green park, fat French babies play in the shade of the trees. . . . Vietnamese police comb through a block of straw shacks in the suburb of Giadinh looking for three Vietminh terrorists. . . . Six nuns glide in black-robed pairs past the great French cathedral in the Place de Pigneau de Behaine. . . . On an informer's tip, plainclothes men of the Vietnamese Sûreté unearth a hoard of Vietminh weapons in the stockrooms of a fashionable downtown lacquer and silver shop. . . . A block away half-naked Vietnamese urchins stand transfixed before a window display of pink-cheeked French dolls.

French women in wisps of bathing suits bake their tanned bodies by the green pool of the Cercle Sportif. . . . A Vietminh grenade kills three men on the terrace of a restaurant on Boulevard Charner. . . . At a formal reception in the palace of the French High Commissioner, four Vietnamese and French officials conceal mutual distrust under a verbal minuet of exquisitely phrased courtesies. . . . Armed with tommy guns, a patrol of Senegalese slouches slow and cat-eyed down a side street off Boulevard Bonnard. . . . Six Foreign Legionnaires ride down the Street of Sailors singing a German song. . . . Across the Saigon River, mortars boom.

Battles are planned, fortunes are made and revolution is plotted in this rich and handsome city once known as the "Pearl of the Orient," now the focus of a war in which nationalism, colonialism and communism are inextricably confused.

To the casual eye, the predominant aspect of Saigon is peaceful. Several million people live in this great metropolis stretched in endless summer along the banks of the Saigon River about thirty miles from the sea. An unimportant village of palm trees and straw shacks until the French occupation of Cochin China in 1862, it developed, like Shanghai, into a prosperous commercial center through the impetus and direction of Western economic exploitation. Through the port of Saigon a small group of monopolistic French concerns funneled French goods and Cochin China's rich exports of rubber, corn and rice.

For many years the administrative center of the French protectorate of Cochin China, Saigon was briefly held by the Vietminh in 1945. Later it became the capital of the French-sponsored Vietnamese Government, established through the French-Bao Dai accords of March 8, 1949. Although Vietnam's chief of state prefers to live fifty miles away in the resort town of Dalat, Saigon is the functioning seat of the Vietnamese Government, as well as French political and military headquarters for all Vietnam.

Except in Cholon, the Chinese quarter, where its residents have re-created the characteristic din and color of their ancestral home, Saigon exudes the atmosphere not of the Orient but of the French who dominate it still. Vietnam's capital might be a busy city in

Provence where Vietnamese have strayed by accident. It was laid out and its public buildings were planned by homesick Frenchmen dreaming, in a dusty tropical village, of Paris, of Versailles, of the Tuileries.

Instead of narrow, winding streets, Saigon has wide, straight boulevards shaded by towering trees perpetually green. There are pleasant little parks and spacious public squares; a great Catholic cathedral raises twin spires in one, and in another, at the town's center, stands a typical French opera house. Not many blocks away an ornate European palace, symbol of ultimate authority in Vietnam, houses the French High Commissioner. Other public buildings in rococo European style fly the flag of the Bao Dai Government—a yellow background crossed by three red bars.

Saigon's main streets are lined with ugly modern buildings, which house apartments, exclusive European shops and big department stores selling expensive French imported merchandise. Dotted among them are innumerable *maisons de coiffeur* and bakeries loaded with French bread; little restaurants offering every French dish from *crêpes suzettes* to snails; streetside cafes where mid-morning customers relax over *croissants and café au lait;* tiny bars where French soldiers, sailors and civilians sit interminably on the sidewalk drinking cognac and Dubonnet.

Saigon's suburbs have a more oriental character, with crowded native stores and flimsy, thatched huts of the poorer Vietnamese. Neat military barracks for the French and Vietnamese troops and the cocky Foreign Legionnaires punctuate the outskirts of town. Cholon is packed with Chinese shops and restaurants; there, too, are Saigon's nightclubs, brothels and great gambling houses where plainclothes men note in little books how much money certain individuals can afford to lose.

At a superficial glance, little in the daily life of Saigon's twenty to thirty thousand French civilians indicates the fears and uncertainties which lie beneath the surface. With no confidence in the morrow, the half dozen great French concerns which for years have monopolized Vietnam's trade are making a killing while they can. Business is good and salaries are high in terms of yearly bonuses; last year one local manager received a bonus of a million and a half piasters, roughly $75,000 at the official rate of exchange. Although the actual value of the piaster is about ten francs, French and Vietnamese can generally manage to remit savings and profits to France at the favorable official rate of seventeen to one. Everyone is accumulating fast for the rainy day after the crash comes.

Merchants, professional men and the hard-working civil servants all still live more comfortably and easily than they could in France. Off the wide residential avenues, houses are roomy, comfortable and staffed with inexpensive Chinese and Vietnamese servants who speak a little French. There is plenty of good food and wine; long siestas after lunch when nothing seems to move in the city except electric fans. There are formal receptions under glittering candelabra; ladies' bridge and "at homes"; movies, cocktail and dinner parties; dining at Le Vieux Moulin, where the rotund French chef seriously discusses sauces and wines with his customers; dancing at Au Chalet, where everyone drinks champagne and watches a new French singer pout her way through a throaty song. There are horse racing and football matches; taxi-dance joints and every type of gambling in Cholon.

For the majority of Saigon's foreign inhabitants, life goes on day after day in the accustomed round. But there exist constant tension and half-acknowledged fear, the moment's sharp uneasiness, the nervous jerk at the unexpected sound. Since the loss of the frontier posts to the Vietminh and the United Nations' reverses in Korea, the exodus of French women and children has begun. The shadow of Communist China now reaches down to darken the air of Saigon.

For everyone knows force alone keeps the European momentarily secure in Saigon. Everyone knows the city itself is a battleground for a savage struggle between the Vietminh underground and the French, an extension of the war being fought over all Vietnam.

Although Tonkin, to the north, is Vietnam's most active military theatre, Saigon lies in a war-dominated countryside. The Vietminh hold large base areas less than twenty-five miles from the French stronghold of Saigon. Vietminh guerrillas raid villages only a few miles from the city. All the highways branching from the Vietnamese capital are guarded every few kilometers by military posts, little brick forts barricaded by fences of barbed wire and sharpened bamboo poles. No cars dare move at night. In the daytime many of the roads are traveled only in armed convoy.

Seven miles from the center of Saigon the Vietminh were strong enough to call a strike at British and American oil installations and fire mortar shells at the plants. Two employes disobeyed Vietminh orders and came to work. They and their families were promptly executed, the head of one woman being placed as warning in the middle of a village street.

Within the city of Saigon itself the sullen faces of the Vietnamese are a constant reminder that an overwhelming majority of the city's population is anti-French and pro-Vietminh. It is estimated that at least 15 per cent of the Saigon Vietnamese are active Vietminh workers.

There are many minor indications of the war of threats, espionage, counterespionage, torture and assassination which take place hourly in Saigon between the Vietminh underground and the police of the French and Vietnamese Sûretés. Every French household is armed, some with a cache of hand grenades as well as guns. Rifles on display in the window of a local sports store are locked in with a massive iron chain. Vietnamese entering theatres are "frisked" for arms. Guards frequently examine shopping bags and bundles of Vietnamese customers walking into department stores. Iron grilles have been placed before some restaurants and house windows to shield interiors against tossed grenades.

Items in heavily censored newspapers give fragmentary testimony to Vietminh activity.

"Yesterday evening a grenade was thrown at the house of an agent of the Vietnamese Sûreté on Rue Colonel Grimaud. No damage was done."

"On the 17th, two Vietnamese policemen fell in a Vietminh ambuscade. One agent was kidnapped; the other was killed."

"In the course of an operation of control in the fifth arrondissement, two agents exchanged fire with two rebels. The two rebels were killed."

No important member of the Vietnamese Government is willing to live in the suburbs or outskirts of town. When a Vietnamese official gives a reception the house, grounds and approaches to them are under heavy guard. Guests arriving in Saigon's motor and wheel-propelled rickshaws dismount a block before the residence while police search the vehicle. Invited to dine with a high Vietnamese official, a guest finds police with tommy guns protecting the residence; the servant waiting on the table has a bulge under his loosely hanging shirt. Armed police protect the homes of official Americans.

An integral part of the Vietminh administrative apparatus for all Vietnam, Saigon's Vietminh underground is extensive, all-pervasive and tightly organized. Its security depends partly on the familiar device by which an agent knows only his own immediate links in the chain. Its power, extending over the lives of a large proportion of the Vietnamese, is greatest in the suburbs.

The control of the Vietminh over the Saigon populace was demonstrated earlier this year when they called a general strike in the Vietnamese capital. The employes of the Government treasury and post office and many of the city's business houses stayed away from work. On another occasion, within less than twenty-four hours, the Vietminh assembled 250,000 people at a student funeral.

At some future date when the military situation in Vietnam has become even more crucial for the French, the Vietminh may well stage a ruthless and ugly uprising against all foreigners in Saigon. To date the chief activities of the underground have been terrorism, collection of minute and extensive intelligence, dissemination of anti-French propaganda and collection of funds.

Probably the great majority of non-European residents of the city pay "taxes" to the Vietminh underground to avoid reprisal in the form of a well-directed grenade or revolver shot. Even some French firms are refuted to pay this "protection money" to the Vietminh.

Vietminh terrorism seems to have two specific functions. execution of "enemies of the people" and demonstration of Vietminh strength in areas most securely held by the French.

"Enemies of the people" run a gamut from the chief of the Vietnamese Sûreté to the little Chinese tailor who withholds some of the tax money he has collected for the underground. The Vietminh have published a public death list which includes members of the French and Vietnamese Sûretés and other key public officials. Earlier this year several Vietnamese Ministers were shot. In April the Vietminh assassinated a key member of the French Sûreté, Bazin, assistant chief of the French Sûreté for all Vietnam. On a downtown street, under the eyes of three Vietnamese police, a Vietminh agent pumped five bullets into Bazin's back and escaped.

Much of the grenade throwing in Saigon comes under the category of reminder of Vietminh strength, as well as such isolated incidents as the burning of the city's public market when American cruisers visited the Vietnamese capital.

A recent large-scale demonstration of Vietminh power was averted by the vigilance and efficiency of the French and Vietnamese Sûretés, which closely cooperate. The Vietminh smuggled into the city a whole battalion of specialized terrorists called the "Volunteers of Death," always quartered in the region of Saigon. According to a careful and minutely organized plan, at exactly 7 o'clock on the evening of Sept. 17 they were to throw one thousand grenades at specific pin-pointed objectives in the city: shops, theatres, bars, restaurants, hotels, streets. Vietminh with automatic weapons were assigned to cover the grenade throwers and block off streets from military reinforcements. Simultaneously Vietminh troops across the Saigon River were to launch mortar shells into Saigon.

The French and Vietnamese Sûretés got wind of the Vietminh plan. Quietly they began to close in on the terrorists. Eighty were caught. The rest slipped out of the city or remained hidden in the underground.

A newcomer to Saigon complained one day that the city's appearance belied its reputation for intrigue.

"Where are all those spies and agents I hear about?" he said to a French newspaperman.

The Frenchman shrugged. "But, of course, in Saigon *everyone* is a spy," he said.

As the head of the Vietnamese Sûreté points out, his organization, the French secret police and the Vietminh all have agents in every corner of Saigon: in homes, offices, stores, hotels, among the *cyclo-pousse* (rickshaw) drivers and the employes of foreign embassies. The Vietnamese Sûreté has an informer in almost every block of the city, some of them also members of the Vietminh underground. It is chiefly through this tremendous net of spies and informers that the French and Vietnamese Sûretés are able to prevent Vietminh activities from seriously paralyzing Saigon's life.

Grenade throwing and assassinations have decreased in Saigon in the last few months. Although this slackening off of terrorist activity may be attributable in part to a change in Vietminh tactics, it is also doubtless due to the ruthless efficiency of a tiny, soft-spoken 55-year-old Vietnamese with close-cropped graying hair, an appealing smile and gentle, wrinkled face—Nguyen Van Tam, for the last six months head of the Vietnamese Sûreté for all Vietnam.

Drastically reorganizing the Vietnamese Sûreté, setting up an extensive system of informers, and working in close cooperation with the traditionally effective French Sûreté, Tam has been so successful that the Vietminh have recently appointed a new chief to rebuild their Saigon underground.

"Without weapons there can be no terrorism," Tam points out. His agents have located and confiscated large quantities of Vietminh guns, ammunition, grenades and secret files. Tam estimates that since he has been in office the Sûreté has captured an average of five Vietminh daily in Saigon. Several of these had been entrusted with the mission of assassinating Tam, who smiles deprecatingly when asked about his personal safety and says he takes precautions—and is a fatalist.

Meanwhile, since no one knows what tomorrow may bring, today the city's normal life goes on.

An old Vietnamese woman shuffles along carrying a live chicken in one hand and a long loaf of French bread in the other. A short skirted Frenchwoman with peroxide hair airs her little poodle. Diminutive Vietnamese urchins sell great bouquets of colored balloons. Two young Frenchmen with tennis racquets hurry by. A Vietnamese schoolboy swings a bottle of ink on a string as he buys a sandwich made of sausage and French bread from a food vender. A fiercely bearded French sailor strolls along with a pretty Vietnamese on his arm, her pale pink robe fluttering as she moves.

Everything looks peaceful and casual on Rue Catinat. But everyone knows the one reality in Saigon is the bitter struggle between the Vietminh and the French. Who will win it, whether it will bathe Saigon in ugly violence, no one can tell.

"Let Peace Not Die of Neglect"

by George F. Kennan

THE AIR vibrates with controversy about America's proper course with respect to Russia. Much of it, it seems to me, is shallow or prejudiced or ill-conceived. It is hard to imagine that ever at any time in history has more error ever been poured out upon a single subject. And one enters with misgivings into this disorder. Where so much confusion lies about, what can we do in a few brief moments to disentangle the snarled skeins, to assemble and sort out and put together again the broken pieces of thought, to bring order out of the chaos—even assuming, which is not proven—that we might have some greater clarity in our own minds? How can we avoid adding to the bedlam, heaping confusion upon confusion?

The only hope I can see of avoiding these pitfalls lies in attempting to re-think our problem, but with a little greater depth in time than we are accustomed to give to it these days.

Thirty-three years ago—not two or three, mark you—*thirty-three*—there was a revolution in Russia. That revolution brought into power a political movement already committed, and long and

deeply committed, to an attitude of hostility toward our own social and political system and to many other things elsewhere which
we believe to be essential to world stability.

It is important to recognize that we did not create that attitude,
nor was there really much we could do to prevent its rise or to
alter it after it appeared. It arose out of ideology and preconception, out of things which were not our doing. To say that it
stemmed only from the Allied intervention in 1919, or from the
way we Westerners treated the Soviet regime generally in the early
years of its power, reflects a very superficial view of the origins of
the Bolshevik movement.

Lenin and his associates, I am sure, would not have been grateful for the implication that their views about the capitalist world
were so shallowly rooted that they could be basically altered by
subjective reactions on their part to the actions of capitalist governments in the period immediately following the revolution. They
would have rejected with resentment and contempt the implication that they could have been glad-handed into the abandonment of ideological principles to which they have devoted their
lives.

This new political power, while not entirely a Russian phenomenon, did succeed in establishing itself in Russia and in bringing under a form of effective and stable control the energies of the
peoples and the natural resources of that area. This fact—namely,
that those energies and resources should have fallen under the
control of a power hostile to Western civilization—was a serious
and disturbing thing. It presented a major complication in the
progress of the West. Those of us who were professionally occupied with Russian affairs in the Twenties and Thirties were very
much aware of that fact. Perhaps that is why we are somewhat
less than impressed when we are told today, by agitated and
vociferous people, that this is the fact and that we ought to be
much more excited about it than we are.

The Bolshevik leaders, in accordance with their ideology, did
their best, in the years that ensued after the revolution, to achieve
the breakdown of non-Communist power in Western Europe, in

this country and elsewhere. They operated Communist fifth-column organizations in practically every area in the world. They unleashed civil wars and revolutions wherever they saw a chance. They sowed confusion and suspicion.

They peddled bitterness and bewilderment and despair. They earned a great deal of resentment in return, and no doubt a certain amount of subversive activity directed against themselves and their system, though nothing near what they claimed. They were a nuisance and a danger to everyone else. In these circumstances everyone else—inevitably and unavoidably—was a nuisance and a danger to them. Their relations with other countries faithfully reflected that fact.

Yet for over two decades nothing frightfully crucial happened in these relations. The Bolsheviks didn't succeed in destroying anybody; nobody succeeded in destroying them. Life was awkward—unnecessarily so—but not impossible. The impact of this Bolshevik hostility and dissatisfaction upon the mellow old democracies of the West led to many remarkable and usually unpleasant things; but it did not lead to war. It was not until another violent and neurotic political movement had raised its head in a neighboring country, Germany—a movement as hostile to Soviet Russia by preconception as Soviet Russia had been hostile to the capitalist West—that major war ensued.

But then, it was not a war between Russia and the Western democracies. The blow struck both Russia and the Western democracies together—like a bolt of lightning, like a reminder to them, from some disgusted deity, of the tragedy and unhappiness of their division.

The war that ensued had two main consequences which we ought to note here. First, by eliminating the armed power of Germany and Japan from certain very important areas of human habitation it opened up new and delicate sources of difference and controversy between the Soviet leaders and the West. These geographic areas, which had been placed by the outcome of hostilities in what might be called a power vacuum, included certain of the world's most sensitive spots, from the strategic and political standpoint. There was no reason to suppose that agreement about their future disposition, as between Russia and the West, would be easy to achieve. There was particularly no reason to assume this, because in a totalitarian regime like that of the U. S. S. R. defensive and offensive motives are always inextricably intertwined, and the anxieties of such a regime for the safety of its own internal power prevent it from reacting normally, or even from speaking frankly, in problems of this kind. All that was known long before the war.

So there these new problems were; and they proved, indeed, to be anything but easy; and because of them it even turned out to be impossible, in the immediate post-war years, to negotiate peace treaties at all. And meanwhile the disputed territories lay there, completely vulnerable in each case, as it happened, to the armed strength of the U. S. S. R., which wholly overshadowed that of the Western powers in the immediate vicinity. And there were many foreign ministers' meetings, many disputes, many disappointments, and much tension—but there was no major war.

The second consequence of World War II that I wish to mention is the establishment of the United Nations. We Americans took a leading part in this. The Russians reacted to proposals from us. You will recall that they were quite emphatic in their insistence on the veto power in the Security Council. This meant an insistence that the U. N. should not be used to settle security problems except where the great powers were in agreement. This applied particularly to precisely the problems we have just noted—the ones arising from the immediate dislocations of the recent war; and this was given indirect recognition in the Charter of the U. N. itself.

Now some of us liked these veto provisions and others didn't; but no one can say that the Soviet Government was not frank in stating its position at the time, or that we were not warned that there might be categories of problems which would be less susceptible than others of treatment in the U. N. forum.

Finally, we should note that when we established the U. N. we placed no barriers to the membership in it of Communist governments. We raised no objection to the Soviet Government's belonging to it, even though we knew it was a Communist government. We didn't ask how it had come by its power—whether by fair means or foul. We didn't ask it to disavow its ideology. We didn't even object to the admission of some of its satellites. It was clearly our view at that time that the U. N. was to consist of both Communist and non-Communist powers.

And we were plainly warned, I repeat, of what logic should have told us anyway: that there were distinct limitations on what such a universal organization, embracing both Communist and non-Communist governments, could be expected to achieve in this immediate post-hostilities period, and that among the things it could not be expected to do would be to serve as an invariably successful forum for the settlement of the problems arising out of war, or for the resolution of the ideological differences between communism and all opposed to it.

Now we have on our hands today a situation the seriousness of which no one would deny. We find ourselves involved in a local military conflict, replete with the most grievous implications, over the problem of disposal of one of those disputed areas from which we required that the power of our recent adversaries be withdrawn. We are indignant over the refusal of Communist China, which is not a member of the U. N., to recognize the authority of that body in the dispute, and over its action in opposing that authority by force of arms. It is worth noting that, whereas we introduced our forces into the conflict, and I think properly and wisely so, the Soviet Government did not. It has preferred to operate, to date, with the forces of its puppets.

Meanwhile, we have come to the conclusion that the general world situation is one which requires a major effort of rearmament on our part and on the part of other Western nations. With this, again, I have no quarrel. I have long believed in the necessity for such rearmament. I think it should have come, to some extent, much earlier. But what I want to get at is not the fact of rearmament, it is the rationale of it. *means to end*

We know many people in this country are coming to believe that war is not only unavoidable but imminent, and that the reasons for rearmament lie not even possibly in the long-term requirements of a relationship with Communist power short of major war, but in some new and recent developments, some new elements of menace in the Soviet attitude, which entitle us to despair altogether of avoiding major war for any considerable further period.

Now this is a very difficult thing to put forth: because anyone who tries to urge caution and sobriety in the judgment of these matters is apt to be accused of having said that war is definitely not coming, that we are not going to be attacked, that our fears are baseless, that we can relax and go home.

Let me make it plain! I am saying none of these things. Of course war is possible. Of course no one can say that we will not be attacked or that major war will not develop from the impetus and the cumulative complications of this situation. Who can say for sure what is in the minds of the Soviet leaders? Who can guarantee their behavior? Who can assure that they, peering out at the world through the muddied and myopic lenses of their bitter and fear-ridden ideology, have not come to the conclusion themselves that war is unavoidable? From such a conclusion anything could flow.

My purpose is not to make a plea for any certainty of a continued absence of major war. It is to make a plea against the assumption of any certainty that war cannot be avoided. It is to plead that before we assume that the world situation has turned basically and irrevocably against the chances of peace we make absolutely sure that we know what we're doing—that we test our views and retest them, putting aside all emotion and irritation and everything subjective—that we take care to see that we are not being carried away here by false assumptions or short memories or emotion.

Let us look carefully at these things which are often cited as the sources of despair.

It is true that the Kremlin is hostile and secretive, and a constant source of worry, danger and annoyance to us all; it has been that way for thirty-three years.

It is true that Western Europe is overshadowed by Soviet armed

comide w/ Kaufman

strength; it has been that way since 1945, and to some extent even earlier.

It is true that Russia has the atomic bomb. Did we then lack warning of this development? Does anybody suppose that we were in a position to assume, let us say three years ago, that they would not have it; that they would refrain from developing it out of some delicate regard for our feelings? I am not saying that these things are pleasant. I am asking whether they are new or unexpected.

It is true that the Kremlin unleashed its Korean puppets against the South Korean Republic. But there is nothing in this fact which is out of accord with the pattern of Soviet behavior we have known for three decades. At no time has there been any reason to suppose that they would not do this sort of thing, if circumstances seemed propitious. The assertion was made in a magazine article three years ago that the main concern of the Kremlin was "to make sure that it has filled every nook and cranny available to it in the basin of world power." There was no objective reason to assume that the Soviet leaders would leave the Korean nook unfilled if they thought they had a chance of filling it at relatively minor risk to themselves and saw time running out on them. I am not trying to justify their action. I am challenging our right to be surprised about it or to call it a manifestation of some "new aggressiveness" on the part of the Soviet Union.

Finally, it is true that Communist China has defied the United Nations. It is true that Communist China has committed acts in Korea which no one can condone and for which its leaders bear the gravest responsibility. If anyone needed proof that these Chinese Communist leaders are behaving hysterically and violently, with a distorted concept of the interests of their own people, and with no understanding at all for the nature and ideals of the non-Communist world, they have it, of course, in these events in Korea.

But the question at issue here is not, and has never been, whether the Chinese Communists were "nice people." The question lies in the amount of damage they are capable of doing, and are apt to do, to world stability. The question lies, for us, in the extent of the threat: in the measure of what we might call the intrinsic tolerances of the Far Eastern area against the effects of these tortured and neurotic attitudes we see in Peiping, and of what then remains to be done, and can only be done, by outside forces, and how much of that is within our capabilities.

Are we sure we have this so carefully figured out? Are we sure we have calculated correctly all the factors involved? China is a strange entity. She is called a world power, and doubtless deserves that designation from the standpoint of cultural and spiritual resources in her people. Actually she is the only country so considered which does not have the wherewithal to manufacture the sinews of her own military strength on a great-power scale. She has to get her major weapons from outside. I dare say that to date a considerable portion has come from us. Must that always be? It is true that China's resources as of today, while limited, are not negligible, and that they are in the hands of people who are foolish and excited and irresponsible. That is a dangerous and worrisome fact. But let us measure realistically the actual extent of this danger; let us be guided by that alone, and not by irritation over the fact that they are foolish and excited and irresponsible. They are not the first people that we have known that were that way, and they will not be the last; and we are not the keepers of their souls.

Now all of this might conceivably add up to the necessity for another world war; but before we decide that it does, let us be terribly, terribly sure we are right. In the old carpenter guilds there was a principle that you should measure seven times before you cut once. Are we sure we have measured here for the seventh time, or even for the third or the second? This is no time to make a false incision. The material will bear no more than one mistake.

A major American weekly recently devoted an article to combating the theory that coexistence with the present Soviet system may be possible. It attacked the Secretary of State for adhering to what it called "this pernicious fallacy." It called upon the President to drive from his councils at long last "all who have sold and fed him on the pap of 'co-existence' with Soviet Communism."

Now these are tricky words, and no one can ever be entirely

sure what they mean. But if they mean what I take them to mean, I would range myself squarely and emphatically with the culprits: with the objects of these attacks and criticisms. What is the phenomenon of extremism and despair with which we are confronted?

Can this be realism, or is it a shrinking away from the first harsh implications of world leadership? Whoever said that world leadership would be easy or comfortable? "Co-existence" with Soviet Communism, as we have seen above, has been possible for thirty-three years. I do not know whether it will continue to be possible for a long time to come. But I would submit that these people who wrote this article do not know for sure that it won't; and in attempting to persuade the public that it won't they have taken upon their shoulders a grievous responsibility and one which I should never wish to have on mine.

They should not try to comfort themselves and their readers with the flimsy pretense that this counsel of despair does not mean war. It does; and if this is the view they are going to take, let them have the forthrightness with themselves and with others to come out and say that what they are talking about is war and tell us how and to what ends and with what resources they propose we conduct that war, and how we are to assure the agreement of the members of a great coalition to a course founded on preconceptions which they do not share, and how a better world is supposed to emerge from the other end of this entire process.

But better still, for them and for all of us, would be not to take this view at all; to admit that the dimness of our vision gives us the right neither to a total optimism nor to a total pessimism, and that our duty to ourselves and to the hopes of mankind lies in avoiding, like the soul of evil itself, that final bit of impatience which tells us to yield the last positions of hope before we have been pressed from them by unanswerable force.

As long as there is a one-thousandth chance that a major world conflict can be avoided—and I hold the chance far greater than that—let us guard that chance like the apple of our eye—let us remain considerate of the hopeful possibilities as well as the discouraging ones—let it not be said of us that we allowed any hope for the avoidance of war to die, like an unwanted and unappreciated child, by abandonment and neglect.

I know that this is the view which has been held by my former associates in the Department of State, and that they will continue, despite all discouragements and opposition, to act on this. If these efforts succeed, the world will have been spared a great catastrophe. If they fail, there will always be time for the other things, the unhappy things, later.

Memorandum
to General MacArthur

by James F. Reston

A FEW FACTS will illustrate how long you've been away and how
much we've changed. You were married at City Hall, New York,
on April 30, 1937, and left the country ten days later. The day
you were married Janet Gaynor was playing in "A Star Is Born"
at the Music Hall. Ronald Colman was starring in "Lost Horizon"
at the Globe. Longchamps Restaurant was advertising a whole
roast beef dinner for 95 cents and Dizzy Dean pitched the St.
Louis Cardinals to a 7-1 victory over the Cincinnati Reds. (By the
way, Dizzy got fired, once, back in 1949. Had a job as a radio an-
nouncer; one of the complaints was that he disobeyed the normal
regulations governing the English language. Kept using the word
"slud.")

Also on your wedding day, the Congress passed the Neutrality
Act of 1937 forbidding Americans to sell or ship arms or munitions to anybody at war. A few days later, Senator Vandenberg
said he was dissatisfied and wanted to make the embargo stiffer.

As a matter of fact, May, 1937, was quite a month. "Gone With the Wind" won the Pulitzer Prize. The German dirigible *Hindenburg* blew up at Lakehurst, N. J., after crossing the Atlantic. The Duke of Windsor married Wallis Warfield, John D. Rockefeller Sr. died at the age of 97; George VI was crowned King and Emperor, etc., etc. Reports that the Germans and Italians were helping Franco in the Spanish civil war were indignantly denied in Berlin and Rome and condemned here as Communist propaganda designed to get us into the war.

Neville Chamberlain replaced Stanley Baldwin as Prime Minister of Great Britain. A little later, just after you got off the President Coolidge in the Philippines, there was what was called a "minor clash" of Chinese and Japanese at the Marco Polo Bridge near Peiping.

Everything hasn't changed since then, of course. The Democrats are still in power, and Gloria Swanson is still flying high, but the "low-priced" car has gone up about $1,000, and who do you think is manager of the Philadelphia Athletics? . . . Wrong, it's Jimmy Dykes. That'll give you an idea.

The big change in Washington is in the isolationist bloc. When you went away, it was a paralytic stroke, now it's an itch. All the factions which existed in the Congress in 1937 are still here— isolationists, the internationalists, the federationists, the air power enthusiasts, etc.—but they exist now in different proportion to each other. It was the internationalists who were on the defensive during that Neutrality Act debate just before you left, but now it's the isolationists who are the defensive minority.

They have lung-power, but little vote-power. At the start of every debate they almost always manage to stir up popular resentments against the expense and danger of world responsibilities.

They are also good at appealing to the natural longings for the simpler days, but in the end they don't get what they want. They have the power to limit, sometimes to delay, and, if they can get the support of the Southern Democrats, they occasionally have the power to hurt the Administration's foreign policy. But they don't have the power to reverse it. In short, the same Congressional battle over what to do with our power still goes on, but the difference is that the isolationists now lose, whereas before you went away they always won.

The explanation is that two wars in a single generation seem to most people here to be enough. The first one cost us 130,274 lives and $21,850,000,000. The second one took 325,464 American lives and by the time most of the veterans benefits are paid for in 1972, it will have cost us about $700,000,000,000. These facts have changed this country. Sometimes some of us forget that; none of us should.

The collapse of British, French, German and Japanese power— in short, the collapse of the only international police force there was—has forced us to shift for the world. And, finally, the obscene picture of the Russians stripping the war-torn nations, like the ghouls of the Middle Ages, who stripped the wounded on the battlefield, has completed the revolution.

In voice and strident pitch, the current debate is not unlike the old pre-war Administration battles with Burt Wheeler and Gerald Nye, but it is important to realize that what is back of this debate is quite different. The imperative need to unify behind an effective American foreign policy not only broke the back of the isolationist power but it created a fundamental political problem for the Republican party. That party has been out of power since 1932. It was blamed at the end of World War I for sabotaging the peace, rejecting the League of Nations and the French alliance. It wished to avoid that charge after World War II.

It wanted to go along with the policy of collective security, but at the same time it naturally wanted to avoid the charge that it was merely an echo of the party in power. The Far Eastern question provided the Republicans with the answer to this political dilemma. They like to complain that they weren't consulted about the Far East but they did not want to be consulted about the Far East. I can remember Senator Vandenberg explaining all this very clearly early in 1946. There must be one or two areas left out of the bipartisan arrangement, he said, for otherwise we would be left without any point of opposition in the whole realm of foreign affairs. You must have heard something of this, too.

Thus, any Administration controversy or calamity in the Far East provides the Republicans with a political argument; indeed, with almost their only foreign policy argument. For the time being some of their leaders are backing your policy, but if the controversy were the other way round, the political hullabaloo here would be almost the same.

What I'm saying is that the noise at present is deceptive. It sounds as if there were a violent party issue over strategy, but it is not a party issue at all, as a comparison of the views of Senators Taft, Lodge, Wherry and Duff will prove. My point is that the issue of where and how we use our power is exaggerated by the approaching Presidential campaign and that the differences over Far Eastern policy are far less grave here than they sound.

The remarkable thing about America in the fourteen years you've been away is not that it has not gone as far as you want it to go but that it has gone as far as it has. There is nothing like it in the history of the world. The British had five or six generations in which to take over, very gradually, a range of world responsibilities which were in no way as risky as those now assumed by the United States. Yet the United States has done this in the fourteen years you have been away. After all, in your farewell report as Chief of Staff, you complained that while the Congress had authorized an army of 280,000 men, it had appropriated money for only 118,750!

Wherever you go you'll find a hangover of the old isolationist days. For example, we still debate in the Congress as if nobody outside the United States gave a damn about what we say. The State Department and the Foreign Service, which are supposed to symbolize our new role in the world, are still full of men trained in the isolationist tradition and determined to maintain it even while operating internationalist policies. The Government, for all its "unification" is still not geared to its new role, and many of the private institutions of the country, from the newspapers to the universities, still haven't caught up with the needs of the day.

Wherever you go, however, you will also find the American people trying desperately to catch up; arguing, discussing, debating, lecturing, traveling around trying to figure out what's the score. The Helen Hokinson character asking the visiting lecturer silly questions about the Montreux Convention may be a figure of fun, but this stout dowager in the funny hat is nevertheless a symbol of an immensely important educational campaign that has been going on in America for the last fourteen years.

There has been nothing like this grass roots adult education campaign on national and international responsibility anywhere in the world, and it is partially responsible for the fact that the isolationists are constantly denying, even in their home states, that they are isolationist.

The points of attack and defense are different now from what they were in 1937. The intellectual Left in America was roaring in the Thirties against the Fascist menace to our civil liberties. It saw the menace of fascism, but in the late Forties it was neither as clear nor as combative in its approach to the Communist menace to these same liberties. Thus when you went away the Left was condemning the Right for its indifference to fascism and the Right was on the defensive. Now it's the other way around, with the Right condemning the Left for its past indifference to the Communist menace and trying to prove still that a New Dealer was half-way to communism.

Some of the great issues of May, 1937, of course, have passed. The sit-down strike was in vogue then, and Roosevelt's court-reorganization plan was paralyzing the whole Congress, but the Republic seems to have survived both crises, and in the confusion Felix Frankfurter turned out to be one of the most conservative members of the court!

Incidentally, if you hear a lot of griping about high taxes and how the Government has paralyzed individual taxes and how the Government has paralyzed individual and corporate initiative—which you probably will in southern Connecticut—try not to smile. There are 20,000,000 more Americans than when you went away in 1937 and they seem to be doing all right.

The national debt has gone up from $41,900,000,000 to $236,-700,000,000 (at last glance), whereas when you went away the

Congress thought a debt of $50,000,000,000 would probably break us. Corporate profits after taxes in 1937 were $4,700,000,-000; corporate profits after taxes in 1950 were $21,900,000,000 and since then they've come through the roof.

Remember when people laughed at Henry Wallace's "Sixty Million Jobs" prediction? There were 60,179,000 employed in March, without counting the people in the armed forces, which was over 10,000,000 more than in 1937, and they spent $190,-800,000,000 on their personal wants compared with $67,100,-000,000 in 1937.

In Washington, though not elsewhere, you will find little sympathy for the theory that private enterprise has taken a beating. In 1937 forty-nine Americans had a taxable income of over a million dollars for the year. In 1949 there were exactly 149. And, incidentally, next time you're in Washington go around and look at the old Bonus Army hangout on the Anacostia Flats. It's all built up into a nice park now!

Nevertheless, there is less security, in the sense of personal tranquility, than when you went away. Never has a country done so much for itself and the rest of the world in fourteen short years, and yet never have there been so many cries that we are in a jam. All the dire 1937 forebodings of war have come to pass, and worse, and yet the United States has survived them and gone on to achievements beyond the wildest dreams of all its "crackpots."

But welcome home, anyway, General. Maybe you can figure it out.

Part 3

REFLECTIONS ON PAST AND FUTURE

IN THE AGONY of stalemate which was to last for nearly two years, observers reviewed various aspects of the war and offered suggestions for policies to follow its conclusion. Economist Sumner Slichter looked at the war's total impact on American life and concluded that the nation could have guns and butter at the same time—and more of both than ever before. Other economists would later see the Korean War as the real turning point where Keynesian theories were finally proven and enshrined as orthodoxy for the next two decades.

Dean Acheson looked at diplomatic prospects, warning that the nation's future policies must fit into "a pattern of responsibility," or the brave decision to hold off the conspiracy in Korea would have been wasted. "Great Empires have risen in this world and have collapsed because they took too narrow a view." Arthur Krock predicted that the Eisenhower administration would make a new beginning in foreign and domestic policy. He expressed approval of Secretary of State-designate John Foster Dulles's desire to use "positive" diplomacy to "stimulate the popular will" inside Russian satellites, and hailed the advent of a new spirit for winning the Cold War and restoring free enterprise at home. With the prospects for a Korean truce finally realized, the focus quickly shifted to Southeast Asia and Japan. James Reston found that American policy was doing better in the Far East than its critics had supposed. American intervention in Korea had given Asia time, perhaps even hope. (The argument would be heard again as the Vietnam War was debated two decades later.) There was a new army of American pioneers working thousands of miles beyond the nation's Western frontiers, offering Asians a new partnership. They might not succeed, Reston admitted, for true "liberation" would have to come from within, but the scene was set for "a good try."

The Past Year and
the Next in Our Economy

by Sumner H. Slichter

IT IS NOW nearly a year since the outbreak of trouble in Korea caused the United States to become a defense economy with a system of controls too stiff for a time of peace but not stiff or comprehensive enough for total war. This is an appropriate time to look backward and forward—to take stock of what has happened to the economy during the last year and to examine the changes and the problems that will confront us in the year ahead.

Certainly the year behind us has been full of surprises. No one, for example, would have predicted that the Federal budget would show a cash surplus of about $7 billion, as it seems certain to do. Although some growth in the output of consumer goods was expected, even in the face of large war expenditures, the increase that has occurred has been highly reassuring. In addition, expenditures on plant and equipment have grown rapidly. This means that the country has been having a triple boom: (1) a defense goods boom; (2) a consumer goods boom; and (3) a capital goods boom.

The year ahead will see many changes. The budget surplus will be replaced by a deficit, unless Congress increases taxes much more than now seems likely; controls over materials will be broader and much stricter and will limit many kinds of production; price controls, which have not yet been really tested because most free-market prices have been little or no higher than ceiling prices, will receive a real test; most important of all, the absorption of goods for defense and foreign aid will grow as fast as the national product, so that the goods available for civilians will cease to increase. No longer will the country be able to expand simultaneously the three kinds of production—defense goods, consumer goods, and capital goods for private industry.

Let us look at the trends shown by the past year and the prospects and problems in the year ahead.

Total Production

The gross national product rose from $294.6 billion (in terms of present dollars) in the second quarter of 1950 to $313.9 billion in the first quarter of 1951, a gain of about 6.6 per cent. About two-thirds of the gain is attributable to increased employment and the remainder to more output per man-hour, which seems to have been increasing at about the "normal" rate of 2.5 per cent per year.

As for the twelve-month period we have now entered, the output of the economy may be expected to increase by roughly 7 to 9 per cent between the first quarter of 1951 and the first quarter of 1952, or between $21 billion and $28 billion a year. The actual growth will depend upon (1) the gain in employment, (2) the increase in hours per week, and (3) the rise in output per man-hour. If employment rises by an expected 2 million, weekly working hours by an expected 3 per cent, and there is no change in output per man-hour, total output will grow by about $21 billion a year; if, in addition, output per man-hour increases by 2 per cent, production will rise by about $28 billion a year.

Defense Production

Output of goods and services for national defense has grown rapidly, but it has absorbed less than half of the increase in the national product during the last year. Defense production today is about two and a half times as large as before Korea. The annual rate is about $30 billion in comparison with $12.4 billion during the second quarter of 1950.

This type of production (including atomic energy and foreign military aid) is now growing at the rate of about $25 billion a year and it will continue to grow at this rate until the first quarter of next year. During the first quarter of next year outlays for defense purposes will be at the rate of about $50 billion a year—roughly $25 billion above the first quarter of 1951. If the output of the economy grows by between $21 billion and $28 billion a year and the outlays on defense continue to rise at the present rate, the supply of goods available for civilian consumption at best will increase very little and it may drop.

However, by the beginning of 1952, or perhaps after the end of the first quarter, the rate of increase in outlays for defense will drop considerably and then will cease, though the expenditures will continue at a high rate for about a year.

The Federal Budget

The budget has surprised everyone. The cash receipts of the Federal Government during the fiscal year, as I have pointed out, will exceed its cash expenditures by around $7 billion. The surplus in the so-called "admiinstrative budget," which excludes operations of the Government's trust funds and which includes some non-cash receipts and payments, will be about $4 billion. In the last quarter of the fiscal year, however, the budget will be substantially in the red.

The deficit, moreover, will probably grow. The present outlook is that the cash expenditures of the Federal Government during the next fiscal year may be as much as $74 billion, of which over $50 billion will be for defense, atomic energy, and foreign military aid. Revenues from present taxes will be about $66 billion to $68 billion. Tax increases are not likely to be large enough to cover the expected deficit. But if the public could be aroused to insist upon reductions in unnecessary expenditures (say, cuts of about $5 billion), little increase in taxes would be necessary.

The Labor Force

The strong demand for goods has caused the labor force, including men in the armed services, to grow at nearly double the normal rate. The increase from April, 1950, to April, 1951, was a little more than a million. The "normal" increase would be around 600,000 to 700,000. Unemployment has been cut in half—from 3.5 million in April, 1950, to 1.7 million in April, 1951. The strong demand for labor in the cities has pulled people out of agriculture, just as it did during the second World War. Today there are 500,000 fewer people working in agriculture than a year ago, but non-agricultural civilian employment has gained 1.9 million. Despite the strong demand for labor, average weekly hours of work in non-agricultural industries as a whole are the same as before the Korean war—despite some increase in weekly hours in manufacturing employment.

These factors make for a growing shortage of labor during the coming year. The shortage will be much more acute as defense production expands. In fact, in another nine months labor shortages are likely to be more critical than material shortages. The reason is that the production of most war goods requires a much higher proportion of labor-hours per ton of material than does the production of civilian goods.

Plant Investment

Industry has been stimulated to increase its productive capacity faster than ever, and additions to plant and equipment are about

30 per cent larger in physical volume during the second quarter of 1951 than in the corresponding quarter last year.

During the immediate future, business concerns are planning further increases in plant, but the Government will have to interfere with many of these plans. Shortages of materials and labor will require that investment in plant and equipment be restricted pretty largely to immediate defense needs. This curtailment of investment will be accomplished in the main through material controls, but tight credit will help.

Inventories

The first effect of the fighting in Korea was to produce a rush of consumer buying that reduced the physical volume of business inventories. In the last quarter of 1950 and the first quarter of 1951, however, inventories expanded rapidly. Today, total business inventories are roughly 10 per cent greater in physical volume than a year ago. Many retailers are worried about the size of their inventories, but in view of the shortages ahead these worries are not justified. Manufacturers' inventories are much smaller in relation to unfilled orders than a year ago.

It ought to be possible to cut the growth of investment in inventories from an annual rate of around $7.9 billion, as in the first quarter of 1951, to $3 billion, or possibly less. This would mitigate somewhat the shortages of goods. Furthermore, by reducing the private demand for investment-seeking funds it would help the Government finance the deficit and the maturities of about $17 billion of publicly held securities during the second half of 1951.

Personal Incomes

Personal incomes have risen about 11 per cent during the last year and in March were running at an annual rate of $23.2 billion above March 1950. Particularly rapid has been the growth of compensation of employes, which increased nearly 20 per cent, from $136.9 billion a year in March, 1950, to $163.9 billion in

March, 1951. Average hourly earnings in manufacturing have risen from $1.453 in June, 1950, to $1.574 in April, 1951. Nevertheless, only about half of all employes have received general wage increases since June of last year.

The prospects are that wage and salary payments will rise by $20 billion to $25 billion a year. About $11 billion to $12 billion of this increase will come from the expansion of employment and the increase in weekly hours of work. About $10 billion or more will come from wage increases. It will be harder to hold down wages in the next year than in the year just past. The half of the wage and salary workers who have not yet had wage advances will expect increases. The Government may take a strong stand against wage increases that exceed the rise in the cost of living, but this is unlikely. The prospect is that the Wage Stabilization Board will prefer not to risk provoking strikes. During the next year wage increases will probably be the most important single inflationary influence in the economy.

Profits

Corporate profits have fallen. In the first quarter of 1951 they were about 22 per cent less than the quarter just preceding the Korean war. This statement will surprise many people because most corporations have been reporting considerably larger earnings than last year. The published reports of most corporations, however, are misleading because they count a rise in the cost of replacing inventories as a profit! This prevalent error in accounting practice caused the annual rate of profits in the first quarter of 1951 to be overstated by $9.5 billion. Profits have been cut by the large increase in corporate income taxes. The corporate income tax liability today is $9.5 billion greater than a year ago.

Reported profits in most industries will drop in the next year, partly because wage rates will rise more than most prices and partly because many companies will be engaged in Government contracts that are less profitable than ordinary business. But real profits will hold up much better than reported profits. The reason is that the prices of raw materials will probably not advance as much as in the last year.

Consumption

The movement of consumption has been erratic, with a tendency for consumer buying to rise when the war news is bad and to fall when it is good. In the first three months after the war started, the physical quantity of goods purchased by consumers rose 4.5 per cent above the previous three months—to an all-time record. In the last quarter of 1950 consumption dropped almost to the pre-Korean rate, and in the first quarter of 1951 it was a little more than 1 per cent above the quarter just prior to the outbreak of fighting in Korea. Money outlay for consumer goods has risen rapidly, and in the first three months of 1951 was more than 10 per cent above the rate before Korea. This, however, has reflected almost entirely the rise in prices, not an increase in the supply of goods.

For the next nine to twelve months the quantity of consumer goods will not increase. Early next year, however, the over-all increase in production should begin to exceed the increased absorption of goods by defense. Hence an advance in the standard of living will again be possible. This assumes that the development of new emergencies does not compel an enlargement of the defense program.

Savings

The rate of personal saving has moved up and down in the opposite direction to consumption expenditures. There have been striking and important changes in the components of personal saving. Most conspicuous has been a marked disposition on the part of individuals to hold cash and bank deposits—individual holdings of currency and bank deposits rose $5.3 billion in the last half of 1950. Saving in this form has the greatest likelihood of aggravating inflation in the future because cash and bank deposits are easily spent. Personal saving has not taken the form of purchases of E bonds—indeed, during the nine months following the outbreak of the Korean war redemptions of E bonds exceeded purchases by $799 million.

During the next year personal saving will increase, probably by substantial amounts. The explanation is simple—personal incomes, as I have pointed out, will rise by $20 billion to $25 billion a year before taxes or about $16 billion to $20 billion after taxes, but the supply of consumer goods will remain virtually unchanged. The extent to which savings increase will depend upon how much prices rise.

It is conceivable that the scramble for goods will cause prices to rise so much that there is *no* increase in personal saving, but this is unlikely. One reason is that personal indebtedness (consumer credit and personal mortgage indebtedness) has increased over $35 billion during the last five years, and individuals will undoubtedly make substantial repayments on this indebtedness. Another reason is that the choice of goods will be less satisfactory than usual.

The preference for cash and bank deposit savings is likely to continue during the next year. Cash and bank deposits, however, are the kind of assets which are most likely at some later date to be converted into goods. In order to discourage the growth of built-in inflation in the form of accumulations of cash and bank deposits, the Government should endeavor to persuade individuals to convert a substantial part of their personal savings into Government securities. This will require (1) building up a sales organization that is able to do a house-to-house job of selling, and (2) offering securities that are well adapted to the needs of small savers.

Prices

The index of wholesale prices rose 16.7 per cent between June and February, but since February there has been virtually no change in the general level of wholesale prices. The consumer price index in

April was 8.2 per cent above last June. The principal immediate cause for the rise in prices, it is important to note, has been a speed-up in the turnover of money which is nearly 15 per cent above last year. Although prices were temporarily frozen on Jan. 25, the ceilings have thus far had relatively little effect except in some wholesale markets, because they have been above market prices. The rise in prices has been retarded by four principal influences: (1) the increase in production available for civilian use; (2) the lag of the wages of about half of the labor force behind the rise in the cost of living; (3) the cash surplus in the Federal budget; and (4) the restraints on consumer credit.

The probable movement in prices is the greatest uncertainty in the whole outlook for the next year. Even though savings increase substantially, the upward pressure on prices will be strong. The demand for goods will put price controls to the test.

Government officials have asserted that rationing will not be necessary because the supply of goods will be ample. Such statements are in error. Price controls are a way of reducing prices below the point at which supply and demand are equal—in other words, they are a way of assuring that supply is less than demand. Consequently, *some* kind of rationing is inevitable. If the Government does not institute rationing, suppliers will have to ration their customers.

Marriages

The war in Korea is stimulating marriages, just as did the second World War. In the first three months of 1951 there were 19.5 per cent more marriages than in the corresponding months of last year. It is uncertain how long the increase in marriages will continue because the number of single adults is considerably less today than a few years ago. Nevertheless, the increase shows no sign of stopping—marriages in March, 1951, were 34.7 per cent greater than in March, 1950. The increase in marriages is an important business fact because it means that a future demand is being built up for houses and many household articles.

Many people express the fear that the huge expenditures on defense are undermining the economic strength of the country. A good way to gain light on this question is to ask what the economy will be like a year hence if the expected trends occur. A year from now the United States will have more plant and equipment than ever before; a larger proportion of the people of working age will be employed; a larger proportion of the adult population will be married; personal indebtedness will be a little lower than it is today. Personal incomes will be about 10 per cent higher.

Personal holdings of cash and bank deposits will be higher than today; the price level will be higher probably by 5 to 10 per cent; the wages of union workers will rise a little faster than prices and the wages of other workers not quite so fast. If the price level rises by 5 to 10 per cent the debt of the Federal Government (though larger in absolute terms than today) will be a little lower relative to incomes. The average rate of interest on the debt, however, will be higher. Hence, the burden of the debt, as measured by the relation of interest to incomes, will probably be larger, but not much larger.

These changes certainly do not, on the whole, indicate a weakening of the economy because they mean that the economy will be better able than ever to produce a high standard of living. The principal question suggested by these developments is whether the tendency for personal incomes to outrun the supply of consumer goods, the drop in personal indebtedness, and the rise in personal holdings of cash and bank deposits are laying the foundation for a serious inflation that will eventually end in a collapse.

This danger is by no means remote. As people accumulate more and more liquid assets their desire to convert them into goods will gradually become stronger. The problem of controlling prices in 1952 will be aggravated by the large maturities of E bonds in that year. I believe, however, that a runaway inflation can be avoided. Some time early in 1952 the growth of the national product will begin to exceed the increase in defense expenditures. As more goods become available for the civilian economy the danger of inflation will not be over but the upward pressure on prices will be diminished.

When one examines the inflation that occurred between 1946 and 1948, one discovers that it was made possible largely by a rapid increase in indebtedness of individuals and business enterprises and by a rapid rise in the turnover of money. But during all or most of the period between 1946 and 1948 the country lacked effective arrangements for restricting the expansion of bank credit. Today the arrangements for controlling credit are not perfect but they are far better than they were between 1946 and 1948. It would be desirable, however, to reduce the danger of a disorderly rise in prices, either now or a year or two later, by persuading individuals to convert a considerable part of their recently acquired cash and bank deposits into private or Government securities.

What Is the Present?
What of the Future?

by Dean Acheson

AT THIS critical moment in history, it is perhaps useful for us to take a long and searching look at the essential character of the times and the struggle which confronts us—to determine what exactly is this critical present in which we live and what attitudes we should adopt in the hope that the future will be less critical.

In an effort to learn about the present, I have had some twenty or thirty important monographs in the Library of Congress examined from three points of view. One was to find out when our serious writers on foreign affairs thought the present situation began. When is "present," in other words? The second thing was, what do these authors believe to be the common characteristic, or what is the outstanding characteristic, of the present, as distinct from the past or the future? The third was, what are the essential steps recommended for dealing with the present?

Let's take first of all when the present situation began. When is "present"? One writer says the present situation began in 1905 with Japanese victory over the Russians in the Russo-Japanese

War. Another writer says it began with the conference at Yalta. Another says it began with General Marshall's mission to China in 1945-46. Another says it began with the invention of the airplane.

Another says it began with the great upsurge of population which took place when modern medicine checked the death rate of the last century. Another one, who is not quite so modern, says it began with the Protestant Reformation! Another says it began with the collective action taken against aggression in Korea. Another, a medievalist, says it began with the Portuguese exploring the Senegal River 500 years ago. Another says the "present" began with the dropping of the atom bomb.

The only point in common that we can find in all these writings is that the present is upon us now. All we know is that we are in the present, but when it began we cannot tell. We can say that there is no one moment when it began. We can say that there will probably be no one moment when it will end. But it is with us. Human experience is not like a book; it is not written in chapters.

Second: What is the fundamental quality of the present? How do you tell the present? How do you know something is present and is not characteristic of the past? We come upon these theories. One is that the fundamental quality of the present situation is that it is a contention between great powers over the control of territory and that in this contention between great powers ideological differences not only are secondary but really obscure the real meaning of the present time. Another writer says that the fundamental characteristic of the present is that it is a conflict between ideologies and that the old conflicts of states about territory have nothing to do with the present.

Another says that it is fundamentally a struggle between the rule of law, imposed in the classic conception of the state, and a conspiracy, on the other hand, which is the revolt of men against the state. Another says that it is the struggle between the awakened peoples of Asia and the decadent peoples of the West. Another says that the fundamental quality of the present situation is that nations have tended to renounce the healthy interest in national self-interest and have run off after the will-of-the-wisp of collective security. Another one says that the quality of the present is that nations have not renounced their interests in national security and have failed to set up collective security in a world commonwealth.

All that we get out of these analyses of the quality of the present is that struggle is at the heart of the times in which we live, that the times in which we live are onerous, but that there is hope for mankind if we will keep our minds on the heart of the problem.

Now we come to the third thing that I asked to have looked up in these monographs: What is the line of action necessary to deal with the present situation?

One writer says that we must recognize that what we are involved in is the struggle for the minds of men and that we must spend vastly more money on that and not waste our funds on economic or military expenditures.

Another one says that the minds of men are trivial things at best, and that the minds of men follow their stomachs and, therefore, the thing to do is to concentrate on economic activities, and intellectual and ideological results will follow. Another writer says military power is the only thing that counts in our time—forget all this nonsense about propaganda and economics and concentrate on the military problem. Another one says that the real heart of the matter is a struggle for power as based upon position and therefore what we must do to settle the contention of our times is to come to agreement dividing the world into power areas. Another one says that the heart of the matter is to get away from the outmoded ideas of national sovereignty and go in for world government so that all differences between nations will be mere partisan friction, and war, if there ever is any war, will become merely small civil disturbances.

Summing up all of this, what you get out of the people who are writing most seriously about our time is that there is no sovereign remedy; that there is no one course to pursue; that there are many courses, many attitudes, which we must take. I think this is a conclusion which is inherently sensible, that there is not any one characteristic of our time, there is not any one answer to it. It has many characteristics and there must be many answers to it.

I venture to put down here then some of the attitudes which seem to me essential for us to have in mind as we take up the problems which confront us.

The first attitude which seems to me essential is the recognition that, whenever the present began and whenever the present will end, it will be with us for a very long time. We cannot escape the problems of the present—except by death or defeat. We must be willing to deal with these problems a very long time and to reduce them to manageable proportions. If we will get that firmly in mind, we will begin to get over the impatience which leads people to try to find magic solutions.

A second attitude which we must have in mind therefore is that there is no single, narrow approach to solving all our present difficulties. We must use all means at our hand, whatever they are, and not say that one is the answer, or one or two are the answers. If, for instance, we should take the views of those who urge that propaganda is the sole necessary weapon to survive and win in the modern world, we easily could find ourselves in the ridiculous position where we have all the people of another nation on our side, but those people are politically organized as an effective opposition to us.

To a very large extent—not completely, but to a very large extent—that is the situation which exists in China. I believe that the vast masses of the people in China are sympathetic to the United States, and yet those masses of people in China are organized effectively against us so that they are a very strong opponent. So propaganda is not the sole answer. It is an important weapon, and we must use it—we must use it fully—but it is not the sole answer.

Neither is dealing with governments alone the sole answer. The idea that we can make arrangements with this, that, or the other government, without regard to popular support founded on free consent would all too probably involve us in excessively brittle

alliances. We have a very good illustration of that sort of brittle-
ness in the arrangements which were made between Hitler and
Mussolini; they seemed very fine but they were very brittle, and
when the pressure was put upon them they broke down. As it
turned out, not the nations but only their passing masters proved
to be the parties to the alliance.

We must be aware of both the fallacy of recovery without defensive strength and the fallacy of military strength upon a shaky
economic foundation. These two things are of vital importance.
They go together and they are at the heart of our efforts at the
present time in the North Atlantic Treaty countries. There you
have a community, an important community, a virile one, one
which has come through grave and deep economic troubles and
has been fighting its way up for some time.

Economic well-being is not enough by itself. The countries
which we have aided along the upward road now see that the
situation demands a tremendous effort to build up, along with us,
military strength as well as economic strength. Defensive strength
is as integral to recovery as a fence is to a cornfield. Yet in seeking
to replenish military strength it is necessary to avoid putting too
great a load on our allies or on ourselves, for that matter.

There must be a very carefully worked out balance between the
firm economic foundation and the strong military defense so that
the military defense does not bring down the economic structure
in ruins and so that the economic structure is built up for the purpose of defending itself with its military components.

The third very important attitude for us to take in dealing with
the problems of the present is to avoid overdramatizing any particular problem or overemphasizing it. That is always our danger,
one not peculiar to the United States but common to everybody.
The particular problem with which we are dealing seems to us to
be the overwhelming problem of all time.

Take Korea, for instance. There is a phrase which has been
applied to it which is typical of this attitude which it is important
to avoid. The activities of the U. N. in Korea have been described
as "the reluctant crusade." That phrase seems to connote that

Korea is the place where the showdown between the East and West is going to occur. "The reluctant crusade"—reluctantly the East and West get into the showdown. Now if anything has been important, if anything has been true about the situation in Korea, it has been the overwhelming importance of *not* forcing a showdown on our side in Korea and *not* permitting our opponents to force a showdown.

That has been the whole heart and essence of the policy which the Administration has been following. Korea's significance is not as the final crusade. Collective security is not something which is established once and for all by some dramatic gesture. Collective security is like a bank account. It is kept alive by the resources which are put into it.

A fourth attitude which I think is important for us to have in mind is a proper sense of proportion about the problems and difficulties which come before us.

In getting the proper sense of proportion about our difficulties, the first thing that we must do is to understand that the present situation is a great deal more serious than the United States as a whole has yet come to realize. We must understand that the Soviet Union is a much tougher adversary than the United States has yet realized. We must not only understand that, but we must understand something else, and that is that the Soviet Union is not the only difficulty that we have. Behind and beyond the Soviet Union, and our problems with the Soviet Union, lie other difficulties, perhaps even greater. The important thing about our actions in the present is that we must so act in dealing with the immediate difficulty that we manage also the more long-range ones.

Twice in our lifetime we have dealt with problems before us as though the solution of the problems was the solution of all problems. We dealt with the Kaiser as though the defeat of the Kaiser was the defeat of all such menace to the world. And yet there immediately grew up after that Hitler and Tojo. Then we dealt with Hitler and Tojo, and then we found looming behind them Stalin and the menace of communism and the Soviet Union.

Now what lies behind the Soviet Union? I see two problems. I am not saying these are caused by the Soviet Union, but I am saying that here are problems which we must reduce to manageable proportion in our dealing with the present. One is the awakening of the vast populations of Asia, populations which are beginning to feel that they should have and should exercise in the world an influence which is proportionate to their numbers and worthy of their cultures.

That force is a force which can be turned to good, or it can be a force which can rend to pieces a world which has imprudently managed its immediate problem and which finds itself weakened, perhaps shattered, in facing these upsurging forces of Asia. Therefore, in thinking about the Soviet Union, we must think about this shadow on the rock behind it. We must manage our difficulties so prudently that we have strength and initiative and power left to help and guide these emerging forces so that they will not turn out to be forces which rend and destroy.

In addition to the emergence of these peoples of Asia with the ambitions and possible power—which has to be thought about in relation not only to the existing power but also to the power which might be left after some imprudently inaugurated struggle had torn the Western world apart—there are the great problems of the world's growing hunger, of its growing numbers, of its deficient knowledge of the very elemental methods of staying alive.

These are the problems, these are the shadows on the rock behind the Soviet Union, of which we must never lose sight.

We must not for one second allow any development which may occur in Korea to lull us into a belief that now we have turned the corner, and now things are going to get better, and therefore we do not need to make the effort which we have been making. I think we need to make it even more than we made it before. We have held off this conspiracy against us, and we have some time now which, if used wisely, will give us the power and give us the union with powerful allies which can deter World War III.

If we do not do that, if we allow ourselves to be lulled by Korea, I can assure you that we will be hit within the next six months to a year with a much tougher blow somewhere else. If we do not make the efforts now, we will be unprepared for that blow. We may completely deter it if we now all bend together every effort we can to going forward with the program.

We must believe that time is on our side. I concede that in saying this there is an element of faith. There is an element of faith because I believe that we are people who act. Time is not on our side if we merely sit in the shade and fan ourselves. Time is on our side if we go to work. We can do much in time. We can strengthen ourselves, we can strengthen our allies. We have a vast productive power which is now not harnessed, much greater than those opposed to us. There is much we can do and, if we will do it, time is on our side. If we don't do it, it is not.

There is one last attitude which I should like to stress, and that is that we must deal with these problems within a pattern of responsibility. I mean that we must act with the consciousness that our responsibility is to interests which are broader than our own immediate American interests. Great empires have risen in this world and have collapsed because they took too narrow a view. There is no divine command which spares the United States from the seeds of destruction which have operated in other great states. There is no instruction to that one of the Fates who holds the shears that she shall withhold them from the thread of life of the United States.

We must operate in a pattern of responsibility which is greater than our own interests. We cannot yield to the temptation, because we are virile and enthusiastic, of thinking that, because we believe a thing, it just must be right. We must not confuse our own opinions with the will of God.

We cannot take the attitude that we will coerce nations, that we are so right that if they do not do exactly what we want them to do we will withhold economic aid, or we will withhold military aid, or we will do this, we will do that. If we take that attitude, then we are creating a relationship indistinguishable from that which exists between the Soviet Union and countries associated with it. That must never be our attitude. We are the leader. But we will continue to be accepted as the leader only if other countries believe that we know today what Thomas Jefferson was talking about when he spoke of the need of paying a decent respect to the opinions of mankind.

"We Can Prosper Without War Orders"

by J. K. Galbraith

WITHOUT DOUBT the most damaging charge made against the United States in recent years is that we cannot afford real peace. The argument, which any reasonably perceptive visitor to Western Europe has almost certainly heard, runs something as follows: The American economy is notoriously unstable and accordingly must be propped up by sizable Government expenditures. The Marshall Plan, for all the fine sentiment in which it was draped, was really a way of keeping the United States prosperous. Rearmament, which has now taken its place, is also necessary for maintaining full employment (and also high profits) in American industry. Thus American foreign policy is really the handmaiden of domestic economic policy. It can't seriously seek alleviation from world tensions, for that would put the domestic economy into a frightful tailspin.

The instinctive reaction of most Americans to this argument, no doubt, is to dismiss it as Communist propaganda, which, in its major inspiration, it undoubtedly is. To shrug off this unpalatable

From the *New York Times Magazine,* September 21, 1952, copyright © 1952 by The New York Times Company.

attack in such fashion, however, seems to me less than wise. Apparently it has swayed a good many people who agree with the Communists on little else. And the simple assertion that we couldn't possibly have a depression is no answer.

We had a serious and exceedingly intractable depression in the Thirties, as almost every literate adult in the world must know. People, especially economists, who have said that such misfortunes cannot recur—who have coined phrases about "new high plateaus"—have often spent the rest of their lives wishing they hadn't spoken. It is time that we dealt plainly with the charge.

The first part of the indictment—namely, that rearmament and military aid are really inspired by the need to prop up the American economy—can be disposed of rather quickly.

To believe it one must also believe that there have been no acts of aggression against the West and, particularly, no invasion of South Korea, for, clearly, it was these that precipitated rearmament. One must also forget the enthusiasm with which the United States disarmed in 1945-46 when peace looked possible and a serious depression exceedingly probable. One must also ignore the fact that, so far, the cost of rearmament in the United States has been paid out of current taxes—were rearmament only for the sake of maintaining output and employment we would be financing it by borrowing. Finally it must be believed that the United States Government, a rather blunt instrument on most matters, has in this instance been able to pull off a giant public works program in strict military disguise, and that we have become so docile as to allow a trick of these proportions to be perpetrated before our eyes.

Such is the argument that we have been arming to keep the economy afloat. The capacity for belief is considerable in our time, as much sad experience has shown, but acceptance of this doctrine must require considerable determination.

If domestic economic necessity has no bearing on armament and defense, it follows that we accept the threat of depression, however grave, if that is the price of peace. There can surely be no doubt that we would do so. In the great issues of war, peace and survival the stability of the American economy is only a detail.

There can be few who could think otherwise. To those unimpressed by the moral issues, it should still be evident that selling apples on New York sidewalks is preferable to being interred under them.

It is still worth inquiring, however, whether a depression is indeed the price that we (and the rest of the democratic world which would certainly share our misfortune) would have to pay for peace.

Unfortunately the possibility of depression, in the event of a dramatic reduction in arms budgets cannot be dismissed as an idle bogy; if it could, the threat of this misfortune would not be serving the Communist cause so well. As I have noted, the depression of the Thirties is impressively on the record. In all of the years since then, moreover, we have had sizable military outlays. (Even at their post-war low in the fiscal year ended June, 1948, military outlays were somewhat greater than all Federal spending in the pump-priming days of the New Deal.)

There are also dangers in the sheer vigor which the economy has displayed since 1945. Expansion has required a large volume of investment which has been sustained in turn by a high rate of saving. Were peace to lead to a general cutback in private investment while savings for the sake of personal security continued to increase, there could easily be trouble.

There might not be trouble—the robust optimists may be right —but the honest course is to concede the worst. It is more important to see how bad that worst might be, and to distinguish between such a short-run or temporary slump, should it occur, and the factors shaping the long-run strength of our economy.

Within the limits of certainty that the uncertain subject of economics allows, two things can be said of the kind of depression that might follow even the most dramatic cutback in military expenditures. First: there is no chance of another disaster like that of 1929. Second: a good deal more could and would be done about it.

The list of misfortunes of the early Thirties which could not recur is impressive. Between 1929 and 1932, for example, farm incomes and prices fell spectacularly. Farmers were heavily in debt and perhaps a million of them lost their farms. All had to cut their ordinary spending severely. By contrast, farmers are now exceedingly solvent; mortgage debt amounts only to about $6 billions as compared with $10 billions in the smaller economy of 1929. Above all, any drop in farm prices and farm incomes would now be checked by Government support prices which farmers and their Congressmen have taken care to see are far above depression levels.

Similarly, the unions would now be able, as they were not twenty years ago, to prevent competitive wage cuts—a policy for which President Hoover pleaded without success in the early Thirties. A substantial body of economic opinion would now also agree that resistance to such cuts in purchasing power is proper anti-depression policy.

In the Thirties the worker who lost his job was dependent on his own savings or meager public and private charity. Unemployment compensation now provides a floor, albeit a rather low one, under his standard of living and hence his spending. With deposit insurance there would be no frantic runs on the banks or frenzied hoarding of cash. A depression would undoubtedly bring some business insolvencies, including some, no doubt, in surprising places. However, no one can suppose that either corporate financial structure or home finance are as vulnerable now as they were left by the strange fiscal aberrations of the great Bull Market.

Finally, broader income taxes have the effect of automatically reducing tax liability as incomes fall and thus releasing income for private spending. It is doubtful if many Europeans or all Americans realize how much stability has been built into the American economy in the last twenty years.

The chances for positive action to check a slump have also been greatly improved. In the event of a sharp cutback in military spending, it would require no very sophisticated economic advice to persuade Congress to enact a whacking reduction in taxes.

Tax reduction might not be a complete answer, for not all of the income that would be released by a dramatic reduction in taxes would be spent. The strong saving instinct of the American people would govern the use of this extra income while, as noted, private investment might decline. In an economy where these matters are left to free choice, unfortunate choices must be allowed for.

But there are further weapons in the public armory to keep things going. A vigorous housing and public works program would be in order. So would a liberalization of social security and, perhaps, a further tax abatement for the explicit purpose of sustaining private purchasing power.

All of this concerns what economists once called the short cycle, the immediate consequences of a shift from a military to a peacetime economy. What of the longer perspective? Can the United States continue to find a peaceable outlet, year after year and decade after decade, for its very considerable productive energies?

The answer is, "Yes, we can prosper without war orders." Here the answer depends less on economics and more on a broad assessment of social need. It is perfectly true that, by any past standard, the American people in the last five years have been living in a condition of considerable opulence. Moreover, the average family income—about $3,300 in 1950—no longer conceals a vast number below the poverty line. There are still a great many poor people in the United States. (It is slightly more accurate to say that there are still many communities, more of them rural than urban, where poverty is the rule rather than the exception.) But there has also been a very considerable leveling up of living standards in recent years.

It has been easy to go on from this condition of comparative well-being to formulate a theory that demand has been saturated, and many have done so. After all, it is said, when families have all the food they can eat, are adequately clothed, are adequately housed and own all of the standard gadgets, what is there left for them to buy?

The question is absurd. Families with a present income of $6,600—or twice the average—have not the slightest difficulty in spending their money. So easily acquired is the amiable art of spending money that the same is true, though with some increase in saving, of those with three or four times as much. It is reasonable to hope, and possible to insure within limits, that the lion's share of continuing increases in national income will accrue to those who need it most.

In a world fully at peace, the United States could afford a higher level of consumption from its total annual product than in the past. As noted, instability, in the past, has been in some part the result of a high rate of saving and investment on which, in turn, a rapid rate of growth depends. We have become so accustomed to investment and expansion that it is in some danger of becoming a god to be worshiped for its own sake. Like all other things in economics it should be subordinate to individual preference. In a peaceful world, more years of better education, more time for enjoyment of home, the arts, the countryside or, for that matter, going to the races might be preferred to more steel mills to produce more automobiles, refrigerators, television sets and other gadgets yet (and perhaps mercifully) unborn.

Yet it is difficult to foresee any shortage of claims on the savings which a peaceful American would have available for investment. There is much work to be done here at home. Both a growing population and the dynamic of technical change will continue to make substantial demands on private investment resources. In housing alone, there are enormous shortages to be made up. In the field of public enterprise, there are schools, roads, hospitals and slums requiring attention. Peace would not quell the ambitions of dam-builders and land reclaimers—and the Missouri, as we have recently been reminded, is still untamed.

More important, peace would not quiet the ambitions of the hundreds of millions of people in the so-called backward lands who must have the help of the United States if they are to make progress toward better living. There can no longer be any doubt that such progress is wanted. This is a task in relation to which even the resources of the United States are, in fact, pathetically small.

For purposes of this discussion it has been convenient to imagine peace without specifying the extraordinary evolution in restraint and sanity which would bring it to pass. However, no one can properly imagine this happy prospect without some continuing promise by the United States and the other fortunate nations to help the less fortunate masses of Asia, Africa, South America and Europe to escape from their present poverty. For an endless period ahead, whatever resources we can spare will be needed and wanted by these countries.

We have not yet developed the techniques for providing such assistance and this is far from a mere detail. I am not certain that we can provide the requisite funds, year after year in the necessary volume, from budget appropriations. I am even more skeptical of those who say, blithely, that private investment will do the job. Perhaps we will need some new kind of instrument for the task—some extra-governmental authority which will channel resources into foreign investment and in which public funds will insure regularity and provide a safety buffer for such private savings as are made available.

These problems remain. What is certain, however, is that men, machines or their counterpart in investment funds must not and cannot remain idle in the United States when they could be serving the urgent demands of other countries. The moral case for the matching of resources to need is strong even in a day when to make a moral case for a proposition is commonly considered a sign of weakness. The practical case—the case that arises out of self-interest—is even stronger.

One can acquire a spurious reputation for hard-headedness by asserting that questions concerning peace had best be left until the day when peace is more nearly assured. This is poor policy. Certainly there are more immediate tasks. But we cannot allow the world to suppose that we consider these more than a means to an end, or that the peaceful end we seek is something of which we are in the slightest measure afraid.

As Eisenhower Takes Up the Burden

by Arthur Krock

THE MAN who this week will become President of the United States, the thirty-third American citizen to be elevated to the office, has expressed a political philosophy of which the following is a good definition:

"A wise and frugal government which shall restrain men from injuring one another, which shall leave them otherwise free to regulate their own pursuits of industry and improvement, and shall not take from the mouth of labor the bread it has earned—this is the sum of good government."

Dwight D. Eisenhower did not write that; Thomas Jefferson did. But every American statesman, Democrat or Republican, who has kept to the middle-of-the-road in which the founders of the Republic set the Constitution has echoed and tried to practice this public philosophy. And at noon on Tuesday next the Presidency will once again be assumed by one of their spiritual and intellectual descendants, after twenty years during which Jefferson's concept was superseded by a complicated system of planning known as the

From the *New York Times Magazine,* January 18, 1953, copyright © 1953 by The New York Times Company.

New Deal-Fair Deal. The first was the brain-child of economic depression in peacetime. The second was delivered from the body corporate by the surgery of World War II and the "Cold War."

But, before the advent of the New Deal with the election of Franklin Delano Roosevelt in 1932, the collapse of an unrestrained, runaway economy—first in Europe then in the United States—and the rise of national socialism abroad that was stimulated by World War I and its inequitable peace terms, already had compelled President Herbert Hoover, who professed belief in the philosophy Jefferson defined, to expand the functions of government and tighten the restraints on the undertakings of individuals. And these grew under Roosevelt with the growth of the problem he never solved—restoring a "normal" economy—until the free enterprise system was regulated by intricate planning at Washington.

The acts of the European and Japanese dictators that led to World War II, and then to the participation of the United States in that conflict, produced requirements for global combat that extended the period of this planned economy. It was prolonged indefinitely because those in power and their advisers believed that the changed conditions of the modern world compelled this fundamental departure from the political creed so long professed and followed in this country.

After Roosevelt died at the beginning of his fourth term and was succeeded by the Vice President, Harry S. Truman, and after World War II ended in victory over the dictators, the new President attempted to relax the controls on enterprise and on the individual citizens, and to deal with the post-war period as a time of peace. But Roosevelt had totally miscalculated the post-war foreign policy of Soviet Russia, thinking it would be cooperative and peaceful. Among the divided counsels of his military advisers at Yalta he had chosen those which favored the concessions to the Kremlin, as the price for entering the war against Japan, that were to be used to advance bolshevism in Asia and lay the train for the Korean war. At Potsdam, after the defeat of Nazi Germany in 1945, President Truman (whom his predecessor had failed to keep currently informed) compounded Roosevelt's costly miscalculation. Hopeful, at least, if not convinced by Stalin's fine words and behavior, that the Soviets would work for peace and keep their compacts, the new President took the advice of his experts and approved the unfortunate Potsdam agreements. And, in this same mood, he and most of his Administration (James Forrestal dissenting) did not resist the military demobilization of 1946 that the public and Congress demanded and would not be denied.

The direct and oblique consequences of these acts, policies and public beliefs were the loss of China to the West, to which the deficiencies of Chiang Kai-shek's Government made a considerable contribution; a vast increase in the military budget of the United States; the resumption of controls over an economy turned again to rearmament; and the new and costly defensive measures represented by the Greek-Turkish aid legislation, the Marshall Plan, the North American Treaty alliance and its military organization for the collective security of the non-Soviet peoples. Other consequences were the resumption of the draft of citizens for military service; a dizzily mounting public debt and deficit for the United States; and finally the intervention by force of the United Nations in Korea to repel and punish the Bolshevist aggression from the North that expanded into war between the world organization and Communist China.

But this intervention, whether or not historians will conclude that acts and statements of the Administration led the Bolshevists to believe that the United States and the United Nations would resist the North Korean attack with words only, was Truman's courageous proof to the Kremlin that its unopposed aggression was at an end and that the West would fight for its principles as well as for its security.

This was the economic and political situation of the United States when General Eisenhower campaigned for President on the Republican ticket against Gov. Adlai E. Stevenson of Illinois, who was drafted by the Democratic convention after President Truman declined to accept renomination. And this is the economic and political situation that will confront President Eisenhower, his Administration, Congress and the United Nations when, at noon next Tuesday, the General takes the oath of office and proceeds to seek remedies.

The major problems of government created by this situation, which the new President will attempt to deal with effectively and by the guide of his campaign pledges, are these:

1. *How to avert World War III and restore enduring peace.*

The heart of this problem is Soviet Russia. It is as much the conviction of the incoming Administration, as it was the rueful discovery of the outgoing one, that Soviet Russia can be brought to those terms by which enduring peace will be restored only if the non-Soviet world becomes powerful enough to assure the defeat and devastate the countries of the Soviet bloc in joined battle, and to disintegrate their regimes and their economies if the cold war goes on a few years longer. So the United States will continue to match the Kremlin with ever-increasing strength, and use every means to induce other free nations to do likewise.

But the new Administration will depart from the old on the diplomatic, and some military, policies and methods that the latter has employed in its relations with the Russians and their puppet Governments. John Foster Dulles, who is to be Secretary of State, has described this departure as a change to positiveness and continuing policy, from improvisation to meet each crisis as it arises; to diplomatic initiative, from merely counter and *ad hoc* diplomacy; to definite moves within the Soviet satellites, that will stimulate the popular will to shake off the Kremlin's yoke, from verbal exhortations and expressions of sympathy. Dulles has also promised to invigorate our activities in the United Nations; and reopen and make all possible use of the channels of diplomacy in ways, lately abandoned, that often before have prevented and ended wars.

And, important in psychological values here and abroad, the new Administration intends to restore the reputation for competence, patriotism and exemplary personal conduct that the State Department personnel enjoyed without challenge until recent years.

The new approach that is indicated for the purpose of bringing the Korean war to an honorable end, in which the warning against further world bolshevism that was implicit in the United Nations intervention will be fortified, is not yet public property. But it is definitely promised as another change of major policy in the effort to produce enduring world peace.

2. *How to reduce the national debt and the deficit, move steadily toward a balanced budget in the United States, and avert a serious depression when our economy turns again from military to peacetime production.*

The financial and economic burdens imposed on the United States by the post-war foreign policy of Soviet Russia render the solution of this problem much more difficult, even for the "wise and frugal" government that Jefferson described as the best. It is already apparent that, though deploring the heavy taxation of the people, the Eisenhower Administration has placed reduction as among its distant goals. The introduction into the Executive branch of more business men and practical financiers than have ever advised an American President or conducted the affairs of the Federal agencies and departments proves that administrative competence and efficient methods will be relied on to make large cuts in the cost of government as a first step toward a balanced budget.

At the Treasury the incoming Secretary, George M. Humphrey, has assembled a brilliant group to deal with debt retirement, borrowing and spending and other measures of fiscal policy with the same purpose in mind; and, in cooperation with the Federal Reserve system, to check inflation through the regulations of private credit. At the Pentagon, Secretary of Defense Charles E. Wilson is obviously expected to effect reforms in procurement and production that will hold waste to a minimum, increase and improve the rate of supply, and conduct a transition of the industrial machine from war to peace without the public calamities that have attended our economic depressions. For it is apparent that, not only these two Cabinet ministers, but all other high administrators and the White House group, are expected never to lose sight of the anti-depression goal which the new President is determined his Administration shall attain.

The fate of the West may depend on whether the Administration is successful in this effort, that will underlie everything it does. For a ruinous depression in the United States could enable global bolshevism to reach all of its objectives without taking the punishment and risking the defeat of a third world war. It could demolish the structure of collective security in the West, greatly weaken this nation internally and externally, and supplant the Eisenhower Administration after one term with a violently radical, neo-Socialist regime.

3. *How to bring peaceful cooperation between management and organized labor.*

The new Administration is plainly dedicated to a first effort in this direction by amendments to the Taft-Hartley Act. The voters overwhelmingly rejected the Truman record, in which very prominently was a political alliance with union labor that gave it a preferred place in the social-economy of the country, and protected the right of citizens to strike to the point where others were denied the right to work. If labor leaders have learned a lesson from this, a better law that will promote this peaceful cooperation can be the result. But if the labor leaders have not learned, and the business and financial community and the Republican politicians read in the election returns a popular mandate for reversion to the conditions that existed before the passage of the Wagner Act, the labor-management strife may become worse in what will be the most critical post-war period. Even in 1952, when there was a strongly pro-labor Administration that went so far as to seize the steel industry for labor's intended benefit, and break its own inflationary ceiling to satisfy John L. Lewis, there were 4,950 strikes, of which thirty-four were major. And the country lost the production of nearly 30 million working man-days.

This problem is at the core of many others. And among its complexities is the basic difference of opinion as to corrective legislation that exists between some Republican leaders in Congress and influential advisers of the President-elect.

But while these three are the principal challenges of all the talents and good fortune that human beings can bring to public office, many more will await the new President when he has taken the oath and reviewed the parade next Tuesday, when the visitors have departed from the White House and Dwight Eisenhower ponders his monumental task. Some of the rest match the three in difficulty and potential consequences for good and evil.

The cost of serious illness is beyond the power of millions of citizens to meet. The Federal Government must lead the effort to remove this blight on the American social order, but by the different philosophy of the new Administration from the old, it must localize immediate responsibility and handling of the reform. The Commission headed by Dr. Paul C. Magnuson that, at the direction of President Truman, made a survey and report has left these for future action.

How to maintain the United States as an asylum for the more assimilable, the oppressed and the nobly venturesome of all lands, and yet close its gates to the backward people, and those of evil life or who would overthrow our institutions by force, sabotage or perversion, was the objective of the McCarran Act. But many of its provisions are denounced as blind, foolish or subversive of the ancient mission of this country, and General Eisenhower has promised corrective amendments. Some of these are sure to be bitterly resisted in Congress.

Segregation of Caucasians and Negroes in the public schools is now a judicial issue before the Supreme Court of the United States, and it may be that in its decision the court will dispose also of that part of the issue that affects the public schools of the Federal District of Columbia. But the minorities charge that this is only one of the racial and religious inequalities that exist in the country; that in opportunities for private employment, in the use of local facilities and in other ways they are victims of majority prejudice and violence that laws and courts have not restrained. The General has promised to devote himself ceaselessly to ending this condition where it violates the letter and spirit of the laws. But he has made the reservation that he will do nothing not clearly intended by the laws. And since a strong movement to change these laws fundamentally, so that Federal police measures may be taken, is as strongly opposed on both social and legal grounds, Eisenhower has here a national dilemma that has hampered our foreign policy because it has been used effectively for anti-American propaganda.

There are the lands and other natural resources of the West to be conserved for public benefit. Ten articles of this length could not adequately review the problem of how to keep the atomic product superior to that of our enemies in its yield of weapons yet draw upon the uses of peace as soon as possible (and Eisenhower must decide when "possible" is). There is agriculture to be nourished and kept prosperous without ruinously inflating the price of food to the individual consumer. There are other prices to be held or adjusted downward with a minimum of controls and with full security to employment and small industry.

The Truman Administration was very slow to recognize that subversives had infiltrated the Government and slower to take measures against them. It permitted its political opposition to lead the essential attack. Because the Administration stubbornly and long resisted full inquiry and action, some members of this opposition adopted counter-measures from which arose a real threat to individual liberty and courageous expression of unpopular views in this country. The principal employers of these counter-measures are members of Eisenhower's party, with great power in Congress. So among his dilemmas is: How to maintain national security from subversive activities and at the same time preserve the right of Americans to differ from prevailing opinion without becoming the riddled targets of calumny and political, economic or social terrorism.

And at the root of every problem are Mr. and Mrs. Homo Sapiens Americanus. Unless the new Administration can win their support and cooperation, particularly those who perform the functions of political office, all its talents, ideas and programs will not make it successful. Government is politics; politicians are human beings; theirs is the "art of the possible, the attainable"; and no matter how emphatic his popular mandate or how personal his triumph at the polls, a President must always remember these simple truths. He must consider the obligations of politicians to their constituents as well as his own. He must not forget that much, if not all, of life is vanity, and that saving face is as vital to an American politician as to any Chinese.

He may wish to choose the best men for administration on the basis of a rigid slide-rule of efficiency, and he can go far to this purpose—all the way in choosing military commanders and Chiefs of Staff. But he must also admit the party workers to the process of selection, and try to persuade them that the best politics is to give him the best helpers. Especially when a group has been out of power and shorn of patronage for twenty years, as the Republicans have been, the need for preferment is acute; and this cannot be left unsatisfied if the supporting strength from his party that a President requires for administrative success is to be forthcoming.

In this kind of political dealing General Eisenhower has been briefly and recently schooled. His training as a professional soldier did not equip him for it. But in his campaign he revealed both awareness and acceptance of its necessity, though in the demonstration he settled for something less than some of the ideals he simultaneously was proclaiming. There were incidents after his election which affronted Senator Robert A. Taft and the Senator's followers, and seemed to be either the consequence of Eisenhower's inexperience or a reversion to the "commander-in-chief psychology." But subsequent incidents—including his decision not to appoint many military men to civil office—suggested that he learned from these experiences some of the limitations of a political leader, even an overwhelmingly elected President; and that one of the most powerful among these limitations is imposed by vital campaign support, sought and accepted, from party factions other than his own.

That those factions exist after, as they did before, the campaign, presents General Eisenhower with one of his most difficult and continuing problems. For there are views on foreign policy in the Republican party that differed fundamentally from his before he was elected, and they differ still. There are also proposals of domestic policy Eisenhower has forecast on which his party will be divided. And, however "loyal" and patriotic, the Democratic opposition (itself divided into factions, too) is almost as large as the Republican majority; it will oppose his program at many points; and it will try ever to coin his mistakes in electoral currency.

But "head winds are right for royal sails," now as they have always been. And neither grave problems, nor their solutions, are new to the man who in awesome solitude made the decision that was his alone to make: to proceed in suddenly foul weather with an invasion of France that had been planned only for fair.

He may truthfully describe himself as Andrew Johnson did, in his inaugural address on April 16, 1865:

"The best energies of my life have been spent in endeavoring to establish and perpetuate the principles of free government, and I believe that the Government in passing through its present perils will settle down upon principles consonant with popular rights more permanent and enduring than heretofore."

And as Dwight Eisenhower takes up a burden as heavy as any President has shouldered, in a time as critical as any President has known, his intimates are confident, and the country hopes they are right, that he will finish his task in a peaceful world and prosperous America. Then it can be said, as of Mr. Valiant-for-Truth in Pilgrim's Progress:

"And all the trumpets sounded for him on the other side."

Of Equal Importance
—Asia's Second Front

by Woodrow Wyatt

UNDERSTANDABLE PREOCCUPATION with the Korean war has tended to obscure the importance of the "second front" in the Orient—the half-forgotten front of Southeast Asia. But the fact is that the loss of the entire Korean peninsula could not affect the security of the West nearly as much as Communist control of that other vital area.

The stakes are vast. In Southeast Asia are six hundred million people and nearly all the world's natural rubber, a high proportion of its tin, a substantial quantity of its oil, and large quantities of other strategic products. Communist dominion over such human and economic resources would swing the balance of world power sharply toward the Moscow-Peiping axis. From India and Pakistan the Middle East would in turn become highly vulnerable, and Europe itself could be cut off from Australia and New Zealand. As the Japanese demonstrated in World War II, the possession of Indo-China and Indonesia gives the possessor immense power in the whole Pacific area.

Until recently the bitter war in Indo-China had gone on without disclosing specifically any clues to China's aims. Then the continuing invasion of Laos, one of the three French-sponsored states in Indo-China, changed the aspect of what hitherto had largely been a colonial war against a Communist-led internal rebellion. Laos, like Cambodia, is a quasi-independent kingdom, quite separate from Vietnam. When Communist China and Russia gave official recognition to Ho Chi-minh, they recognized his Vietminh as the Government of Vietnam alone; Laos and Cambodia were excluded. Though Ho Chi-minh's troops have now evacuated three quarters of the area which they first occupied in Laos, they still retain control of the town of Samneua and are busily setting up Communist cells throughout a wide area.

Any theory that the Chinese Communists are eager to get back to internal problems and shun foreign adventure is questionable in the light of China's historic attitude toward her southern neighbors. Chinese outside China, though often anti-Communist, remain essentially Chinese in their outlook, even to their contempt for foreigners. In Southeast Asia are a number of Chinese enclaves—in Burma some 300,000 Chinese; in Thailand 2,500,000; Indo-China 850,000; Malaya over 2,500,000 (approximately half the population); and Indonesia 2,000,000.

By Chinese law the Chinese overseas cannot lose his nationality. Recently the Communist Government in China has made arrangements for overseas Chinese to elect representatives to the new parliament that the Communists are constructing in China itself. Clearly the overseas Chinese are valuable adjuncts to any policy of pressure that the Chinese may desire to apply against Southeast Asia.

From Peiping's point of view Southeast Asia now is a peculiarly profitable field for expansion. For the most part, newly independent Governments are weakly in control, easily shaken by outside pressures and internal disturbances. The hideous poverty over so much of the area affords promising material for communism. The prize is a rich one and the winning of it would put China on an equal footing with Russia.

Today, only a combination of American assistance and the fact that the traditions and the ideas of the West are still ascendant, keeps Southeast Asia tenuously anti-Communist. One has only to recall the experience of the last World War to visualize what could happen. Thailand, for example, at that time was on the side of Western democracy. But she also has always bent to the strongest power in the area, and when the Japanese army arrived at her frontier she quickly went over. Just as swiftly, when the Japanese were defeated, she switched back into the Western embrace. If Indo-China were to go Communist tomorrow the pressures to change the shape and direction of the Thailand Government would be almost irresistible. Very probably the "Free Thai" movement operating in Laos, Thailand and Burma would be successful in setting up a government in Bangkok. The Prime Minister is already available—Nai Pridi, a previous Thai Prime Minister of considerable prestige, who is now in exile but believed to be with the Chinese Communists.

Similarly in Burma, still fissured by insurrections which followed her independence, the Burmese Communists could easily set up a bogus government among the Thais in the Shan States, then appeal for "liberation" to the Chinese Communists just over the frontier. To the outside world their claim to be fighting for national independence would be bolstered by the presence in Burma of the Chinese Nationalist troops who have been supplied with American arms brought from Formosa by the agents of Chiang Kai-shek.

The fall of Indo-China likewise would have a deplorable effect in Malaya. Since February, 1952, when General Templer was appointed High Commissioner for Malaya, he has steadily persuaded more and more of the Chinese population to give active assistance in dealing with the Communist bandits or at least to stop helping them. But with the Communists in control in Indo-China Chinese morale in Malaya would collapse again and, with a little outside Chinese assistance, the Communists would become as dangerous as they are now in Indo-China. Few Chinese in Malaya would dare to expose themselves to retribution by cooperating with the Government.

Once Burma had gone the way would be open to Communist domination of India and Pakistan. The morale of the Communists there, already dangerously troublesome, would be stimulated. The Chinese interest in India is pointed up by the elaborate care they have taken to colonize Tibet and to line its common frontier with India with large numbers of troops, something that has never happened before.

Assuming, then, both a Communist occupation of the whole of Indo-China and an unchecked Chinese intention to expand, the outlook for Southeast Asia would be dismal. Peace in Korea would release hundreds of thousands of Chinese troops to push against the weaker parts of Asia. If, at the same time, a large number of American troops are withdrawn from Korea, there is little likelihood that American public opinion would strongly support their being sent right back into battle to assist the small countries of Southeast Asia—particularly if the Chinese succeeded in confusing the world as to exactly what the issue was in any country it threatened.

Since Southeast Asia lies exposed to the threat of the Chinese Communists, what can be done to give it security? Many views of the Southeast Asians on the world political scene seem, to us, unreasonable. But if we are to keep them on our side and to persuade them to mobilize themselves to meet the growing threat to their integrity then we have to take into account their psychology, and do all we can to induce Southeast Asia to help herself to defend herself. Then, and only then, can America and Britain be of help.

One key to the area's defense is obviously Indo-China. The present unhappy situation there is largely a tragic result of France's failure to deal with Indo-China as the British did with India and Burma at the end of the war. The French reluctance to hand over power produced a violent national reaction which the Communists twisted to serve their own ends. The ordinary citizen of Vietnam believes in his heart he can best achieve independence by fighting the French. Yet, it is the Chinese who, for 2,500 years, have been the traditional enemies of the Indo-Chinese. If the French could be removed from the picture then the Vietnamese might be made to realize that the real threat to their independence comes not from France but from the Chinese Communists.

This can happen, many observers are convinced, only if the French make Vietnam, Laos and Cambodia genuinely independent with all speed and progressively hand over the conduct of the fighting to the Vietnamese Army, which is already 200,000 strong (as against the Vietminh Army of 300,000) and which will have 450,-000 troops by the end of 1954. By this process, the attitude of the Vietnamese could be reversed—the Chinese now helping Ho Chi-minh would become the enemy in the place of the French. The West, of course, would have to continue to supply the Vietnamese forces with arms but instead of their being supplied for today's struggle—which the French cannot win because they have not the sympathy of the people—they would be going to an independent country which would have the support and sympathy of the rest of Southeast Asia.

The recent French proposals for further independence for Laos, Cambodia and Vietnam are encouraging. The response has been good in Vietnam and Laos, though the Cambodians are more doubtful. But even now the French qualify their offer of outright independence by demanding that the three states of Indo-China should conduct their foreign policy only by reference to and through the French.

If Vietnam had genuine independence, it might well be possible for the Vietnamese government, if it could not finally defeat Ho Chi-minh in the field, to come to a reasonably acceptable settlement with the Vietminh. Even more important, India would be able to recognize the Vietnamese government, which she will not do today. Southeast Asia can only be saved from Communist domination, particularly if Indo-China falls, if India takes the lead in organizing her neighbors in the interests of her own self-defense, as Western Europe organized herself a few years ago in the face of the Russian threat.

But thinking in Southeast Asia is confused by living memories of colonial rule and the lack of first-hand experience with Communist dictatorship. Southeast Asians are still more afraid of imperialism, of which the French in Indo-China seem to them an outstanding example, than they are of communism.

They are awakening to the realities, but several psychological barriers remain. There is the sympathy with the Chinese Communists' claim that their revolution was in part an expression of Asian nationalism directed against attempted Western domination, as exemplified by the massive aid given to Chiang Kai-shek by the Americans. Southeast Asia does not yet feel that the West has done everything it could have done to insure that the Chinese do not have reasonable grievances.

The Western reputation is further marred by the continuing presence of the 15,000 armed Chinese Nationalist troops in Burma, who fled across the border after Chiang Kai-shek's defeat. Southeast Asia feels that if America, and to a lesser extent Britain, really wanted to have this potential source of trouble with the Chinese Communists removed, they could persuade Chiang Kai-shek to do it.

Again India and Southeast Asia believe Communist China is entitled by the weight of the facts to the Chinese seat on the Security Council. There is some understanding of the refusal to admit Communist China to the United Nations so long as she is actually fighting against the United Nations troops; but there is no understanding whatever of the proposition that once the fighting has stopped, Communist China is still not to be allowed her place among the world's nations.

It may well be that American opinion will find it hard not to continue to resist the entry of Communist China into U. N. But, palatable or not, it should be realized that the longer Communist China is kept out, the more friends will be lost to America and the West in Southeast Asia. Once Communist China is seated on the

Security Council, Southeast Asia might cease finding excuses for Chinese bad behavior and take instead the action necessary to prepare for her own self-defense.

Similarly, the support of Chiang Kai-shek on Formosa by American arms and supplies is seen by Southeast Asia as a potential imperialist threat. Southeast Asians cannot believe that there can be any good motive for aiding what is to them a ramshackle and discredited government which apart from anything else, has no possibility of restoring itself on the mainland of China. They feel that America is using Formosa as a kind of auxiliary military base. While Southeast Asians may not expect Formosa to be handed over to Communist China, they, at the very least, expect it to be completely neutralized in some way under United Nations auspices—perhaps with a plebiscite of its inhabitants, after a period of, say, ten years, to decide its ultimate future.

It is in such ways that the West has a chance to convince Southeast Asia that colonialism and imperialism have completely vanished and that China has been given every chance to behave decently. It also goes without saying that the more economic aid that can be given to Southeast Asia the less able will the Communists be to obtain converts. (India and Pakistan note ruefully that for economic aid they will together get, in the coming year, $94 million as against $2 billion allotted for military aid in the general area of China and $400 million for the military defense of Indo-China.)

With the right background provided by the West the way will be clear for India to call a conference of Southeast Asian countries to consider the Indo-China situation. That conference would need to issue a non-aggressive statement warning China that should she threaten the integrity of any country in Southeast Asia directly or indirectly, then each country in Southeast Asia would feel itself to be involved. It would be a mild form of NATO for Southeast Asia.

That would give America and Britain and the U. N. a clear issue on which they could bring assistance at once if any country in Southeast Asia were attacked even though the machinery of a

"People's Government" had been used. While the Chinese, as the Russians were in Europe, are very willing to extend their empire if they can get away with it without a world war, the knowledge that movements beyond their frontiers would precipitate something far larger than they had intended would serve to keep them in check.

America in Asia:
Time and a Little Hope

by James Reston

YOKOHAMA.

IT'S TRUE what they say about the United States in Asia. We are
dogmatic, inexperienced—an unfortunate combination—flighty,
contradictory and unpopular. But it's only a part of the truth and
not by any means the main part; for America is engaged throughout this vast area in one of the noblest enterprises in our history,
and the tragedy of it is that most Americans don't know it. Even
those American officials who are working night and day here to
keep half the world's population from falling to the Communists
are so overwhelmed by what's wrong with the situation that they
tend to forget what's right. Like many Americans at home and like
almost all Asians, they are so preoccupied with what remains to
be done that they minimize what has been and is being done.

America has given Asia time and maybe even a little hope. Not
so long ago the British and French in this part of the world were
in a state of unrelieved gloom, Chinese Communists were being
hailed by the powerful Chinese communities throughout Southeast

From the *New York Times Magazine*, August 30, 1953, copyright © 1953
by The New York Times Company.

Asia as conquering heroes, Japan was in a state of obedient indifference, and Communist armies were approaching the southern tip of the Korean peninsula.

The situation isn't a whole lot better now but, if progress can be measured in terms of stopping bad things as well as in terms of doing good things, some progress has been made. The British and French now seem to have days when they see possibilities in future plans for Asia instead of always seeing only difficulties. Enough time has gone by so that Southeast Asia now sees not only the power and triumphs of the Peiping régime but its tyranny as well. The Japanese are sitting right up sassing us back in one of the most annoying but encouraging of the world's present anti-American movements. And not only are the Communist armies standing still behind the Thirty-eighth Parallel in Korea but we are beginning to see an interesting struggle between Soviet and Chinese Communists over whose satellite North Korea is to be.

Thus America may be divided, inexperienced, flighty and dogmatic, but the main thing is that we are here—with our power and our optimism—leading, bribing, goading, shaming and occasionally threatening a whole catalogue of countries into strengthening their societies and defending their freedom. The American trumpet does not always give forth a clear, certain note in Asia. We do not always give good advice, or even the same advice—all divisions in Washington having been transferred to the field. Also it's true, as charged, that we meddle in the internal affairs of a whole variety of countries. But Asia is full of politicians who condemn us publicly for our intervention, but proclaim in private that without our interference constructive forces throughout this area would long ago have been overwhelmed.

Despite all the complaining in America that we have failed in Asia, therefore, this reporter reaches the end of the 26,000-mile trip through Southeast Asia and the Far East with a sense of pride in the activities of his countrymen and a suspicion that we may be doing better than we suppose. I cannot, of course, prove the point. All I can do is report what I saw and put down impressions which may or may not be accurate.

Early last June I got aboard the *Maren Maersk,* a Danish freighter bound for the Philippines, Formosa, Hong Kong, French Indo-China, Thailand and Japan. The freighter is slow and I had to leave it here and there to have more time in Korea and Indo-China, but it's a good companion on a reporting assignment, for it doesn't fly over the pestilence or the poor people of the Orient. Furthermore, it tells a great deal about what America produces, how much we are needed in Asia and how we are trying to help.

The *Maren Maersk* on this trip, for example, carried a typical cargo:

For the Philippines: shotguns, rifles and shells for the chief of the Philippine constabulary (the Filipinos are trying to quell a Communist armed rebellion and run an election at the same time); medical supplies for the endless war against disease in this part of the world; replacement parts for American machines brought here during our control of these islands, and a couple of other items reminiscent of the American occupation—twelve cartons of chewing gum for Triad Trading Company and vast quantities of Coca-Cola (there is no truce in the ice-cold war between Coca-Cola and Pepsi-Cola out here).

For Formosa: partial equipment for three new American power transformers (including explosion-proof switches); 5,080 cases of fancy groceries costing $33,776.85, whose consignee turned out to be an American cloak-and-dagger outfit "visiting" in the area; the inevitable shipment of jeep parts; and from the Mennonite Central Committee of Akron, Pa., to the Mennonite Central Committee, 94 North Chungsan Road, Taipei, an almost perfectly balanced shipment—eighty-three cartons of canned meat, four bales of new bedding, thirteen cases of soap, five cartons of Christmas greeting cards, and one case of toys and dolls.

For French Indo-China: more warlike cargo—aircraft ground maintenance equipment; bulldozer and tractor replacement parts; airplane, radio, signal corps, tank and telephone parts; and a considerable quantity of personal parachutes. (Incidentally, you learn something about the practical side of international politics aboard a freighter. For example, the Chinese Nationalist Government, to be sure nobody gets more from America than it does, insists on seeing the cargo lists for Indo-China and all other ports of call beyond Formosa.)

America's contribution to the safety and sanity of Asia, however, goes well beyond the products of her factories. The first island we passed was Marcus, a lonely speck of less than a thousand acres of coral where several hundred Americans live alongside an airstrip to guard the sea approaches to Japan. The first ship we passed beyond Marcus was an American weather vessel. When we were en route from Formosa to Kobe in southern Japan a U. S. Navy PBY plane, engaged in protecting the Formosan Straits, circled us almost at mast height to check our ship's identity. And when typhoon "Kit" was in our vicinity off the Philippines, Captain Peter Labo of the *Maren Maersk* was guiding his ship in accordance with reports from American planes and on maps provided by the U. S. Navy.

The range of American activities in this part of the world is unbelievable. Take the case of Cubi Point, which few Americans ever heard of. This is one of three ridges of the Zambales Mountains, which jut into Subic Bay north of the Bataan peninsula on the island of Luzon. At the end of the war the United States had two major bases near Manila—a naval air station at Sangley Point in Cavite, which is unusable in typhoon weather, and Corregidor, which was smashed by the Japanese at the beginning of the war and has now been recaptured by the jungle.

The United States started building Cubi Point, in 1951, into the Navy's most advanced base in support of airplane carriers in this part of the world. Two years ago Cubi Point was a wild jungle swamp dominated by the Huks. Since then Seabees armed with bulldozers, giant scrapers, hydraulic pumps and blasting equipment have built a 10,000-foot runway out into the sea, taken some 200 feet off the top of a mountain behind the strip, filled in 200 acres of swampland, cleared the jungle, moved and rebuilt the native village of Benikain and built a network of communications between the airstrip and the naval station on the other side of Subic Bay reservation.

In terms of the amount of earth moved, the project was about a tenth as big as the Panama Canal. This base is within a 1,500-mile radius of all the trouble spots in this part of the world—Korea, Indo-China, Formosa, Japan—and with Okinawa it will serve as the main repository of American power when the United States finally has withdrawn from Japan.

Everywhere, from Singapore to Seoul, the American effort is different because the problem is different. France carries the bulk of Indo-China—and a terrible burden it is—but the United States paid 30 per cent of the total military cost last year and will probably carry more than half the total this year.

In Korea, Japan and Formosa, dependence on America is so great as to be almost pathetic. I had long talks with Syngman Rhee, Premier Yoshida of Japan and Chiang Kai-shek. Each in his own way had criticisms to make of American policy and all were asking the United States to do more. But at the same time all three looked to Washington as the place where, if anywhere, they would find security.

America is not only supplying the power which keeps these areas out of Communist hands but supplying the spirit that enables these governments of East Asia to tolerate one another.

The weakness, lack of democratic spirit and hostility toward each other of allied governments here are appalling. There is very little evidence they understand the democratic spirit which underlies American policy throughout Asia, and each is so overwhelmed by its own problems that it has very little understanding or appreciation of other problems or of America's responsibilities all across the world.

The Koreans hate their former masters, the Japanese, and the Japanese have contempt for Koreans. Formosa Chinese not only are suspicious of the British but fear that a revived Japan may try to reconquer Formosa. The Philippines and so-called Independent States of Indo-China are both fighting Communists, but the Philippine Government refuses to recognize the Independent States.

It is therefore wrong to speak of a "non-Communist Pacific alliance." What we have is a series of separate, divided states struggling without much experience toward independence and prevented from falling into anarchy mainly by the leadership and tangible power of the United States. Wherever you go you find Americans either holding the military line themselves, or furnishing supplies, or helping with the difficult business of trying to persuade allied governments to improve their defenses and their institutions.

This is the great untold American story of the post-war era—a story of the sacrifice of literally thousands of Americans who are working out here with young Asian governments.

It is not an easy part of the world for Americans. For a great many of them every meal, every street corner is a crisis. For those of them with young children the problems of health and education are immense. Yet without any great tradition of long-term service overseas, without institutions at home to deal effectively with the problems of education on small salaries, they accept occupational hazards without much complaint.

One finds Americans, for example, working with French and Vietnamese trying to wipe out malaria, trachoma, yaws and intestinal parasites behind the lines in Indo-China, providing pure wells, first-aid supplies and prefabricated hospitals in the Philippines, sending teams of agricultural experts into the south of Formosa to try and grow three crops of rice yearly where only two grew before, caring for Korean refugees in the unspeakable filth and poverty of Pusan, and trying to organize the intellectuals and labor-union leaders of Japan to deal effectively with disturbing pro-Communist sentiments in the Japanese labor unions and universities.

This sort of thing goes on everywhere in Asia now. It is a limited operation, expensive, often poorly run—particularly in the field of ideas—and often misdirected, but in some fields it is having a lasting effect on the pattern of Asian society.

Japanese women are at least partially emancipated by the MacArthur reforms and are not likely to return to quite the same inferior position they suffered before the war. Land reform in Formosa, put through under pressure from the United States, certainly has improved the status of the Formosa farmer. For good or ill, the Independent States of Indo-China have broken with French colonial rule. And if the United States can purchase a little cooperation from Rhee with its billion-dollar Korean reconstruction program, that hard-battered peninsula may finally learn something of civil liberties.

None of this is intended to suggest that America is winning the battle for Asia or even that Asia understands what we are trying to do. Asiatic history, with its inheritance of hatred of the white man, is against us everywhere in the region, and geography is against us as well in both Korea and Indo-China.

Nevertheless, the United States has given Asia an opportunity to observe something new. Asia's complaint against the white man for two hundred years has been that he came to take away, and that he used any amount of physical power to achieve his own selfish ends. Asia cannot say that to America. We have come to Asia not to take away but to give, and while we have used our power to punish aggressors we restrained the use of that power in the hope of achieving a compromise settlement.

An Asia which is in the throes of both civil war and vast revolution may reject this policy of moderation, but there are some indications that it will not. Japan is slowly regaining an independent spirit and will rearm in due course. Relations between Japan and the Philippines, whose cooperation is vital to our long-range security plans in the Pacific, are improving. And neither the Chinese nor the Soviet Communists are showing any eagerness for the time being to try to take Formosa or Indo-China by force of arms.

America has not, of course, "liberated" Asia—only Asia itself can do that—but because we have not succeeded in doing everything, it does not follow that we are doing nothing or that we are failing. There are stormy discrepancies of approach everywhere—among ourselves and with our allies as well as with our enemies. The headlines are noisy with dissensions and contradictions, but headlines are not necessarily the whole of history and the American effort is something more than the goings and comings and pronouncements of our officials.

That effort is something of which every American can be proud. It is the million American soldiers who have been in Korea punishing the aggressors in a way that neither we nor the British nor the French did in the 'Teens or the Thirties. It is the lonely American airmen on Marcus, and the sanitary engineers spreading DDT and digging safe wells in Indo-China. It is the Seabees moving mountains at Cubi Point in the Philippines, and the traveling United States libraries in Japan.

There is, in short, a new army of American pioneers working thousands of miles beyond our Western frontiers, offering Asia a new kind of partnership. They may not in the end succeed. They certainly will not remove in a decade the accumulated grievances and prejudices of a thousand years. In fact, Asia, egocentric as a cat, skewed in body and in spirit, may reject our partnership— which is her privilege—but it is a good try, none the less: one of the most glorious in American history.

Europe or Asia
—Priority for Which?

by Hanson W. Baldwin

A NEW AND urgent chapter in an old debate over our defense policy
—Europe first or Asia first?—has opened with the armistice in
Korea. Which continent should receive priority in arms and equip-
ment, money and effort?

The question has taken on special meaning because of the
change of regime and tactics in Moscow. If we knew the broad
lines of Russian strategy—which front, for example, the Malenkov
regime intends to emphasize—our policy-making would of course
be a far simpler undertaking. But the Russians do not have their
Great Debates in public. Even the knowledge that Malenkov has
been influential in stressing the role of Asia in the struggle for
world communism is not much for us to go on. And initial over-
tures to the West have now been followed by the ominous claim
that the Soviet Union has mastered production of the hydrogen
bomb.

In this country the debate continues in the open. Today, as in
the past, there is an "Asia-first" party and a "Europe-first" group,

From the *New York Times Magazine*, August 16, 1953, copyright © 1953
by The New York Times Company.

and they press their views even while showing some agreement that both areas are of vital political and strategic importance.

Any objective attempt to weigh the relative importance of the two continents must include a summary of the arguments made by both sides, an assessment of those arguments against the background of the present politico-strategic situation, and a comparison of the strategic positions, populations and resources of East and West.

1. The Arguments

Asia is the continent where the bullets have been flying and American boys have been dying; our efforts should be concentrated there, say the Pacific-firsters.

"The preservation of the Western Community and hence the defense of Europe have precedence over all other commitments of the United States in world politics," writes Robert Strausz-Hupé, a Europe-firster, in his new book, "The Zone of Indifference." "If it is not this decision that oriented American foreign policy then its meaning is indeed that of a child's tale told by an idiot. . . . The objective of Soviet strategy is the control of the industrial regions of Europe."

But, retorts the opposition, communism contemplates eventual conquest of Europe through the back door of Asia; there's no use barricading the front door while leaving the rear entrance unlocked. Anyway, say the Asia-firsters—following the lead of Spengler—Europe is a static and perhaps a dying continent; Asia is a teeming, virile, undeveloped continent where the future will be made.

Let's concentrate on the present problem is the answer of those who feel that Europe must have priority. The United Kingdom has the world's second largest navy, the third or fourth largest air force, and a great backlog of technical know-how. Our other European allies furnish military establishments far more modern—and collectively more powerful—than those of the Orient. Titoism already has cracked the monolithic structure of communism, and

Germany, with its great vigor, military tradition, industrial techniques and genius for organization, is the key not only to Europe but to the world struggle.

II. The Facts

Since the end of World War II, the United States has expended about $6,900,000,000 in aid of all types (economic, military and Point Four) to Asia, and about $28,800,000,000 in aid to Europe. The foreign aid program for the 1953 fiscal year allocates $4,990,-114,713 for aid to Europe and $954,448,927 to Asia. The 1954 budget as passed by the Congress provides $2,250,000,000 for Europe and $1,968,000,000 for Asia, including the Near East. The United States exports to Europe represent about three times the dollar value of our exports to Asia, whereas our imports from Asia are about $100,000,000 more than those from Europe.

Today there are roughly 650,000 American soldiers, sailors and airmen assigned outside the continental United States to the Asia-Alaskan-Western Pacific area. There are some 425,000 Americans in uniform in the European area. NATO plans contemplate the assignment of some fifteen to twenty additional air wings to Europe. One additional Marine division is being assigned to the Pacific.

Asia is the continent of today's hot wars; Europe of the cold war. The opposing military forces in Asia number about 1,350,000 on the pro-Communist side against 1,900,000 in the anti-Communist camp. In Europe, more than 2,000,000 NATO armed forces are under arms, facing more than 2,000,000 Russians and their satellites in Eastern Europe.

In Asia, China, the long-slumbering giant, seems to be breaking some of the shackles of the past and, under a tightly centralized Communist Government, has made appreciable progress in two years toward becoming a modern military power.

In Europe, the heresy of Titoism has shaken the Moscow brand of communism, and the influence of Yugoslavia, particularly in the Balkans, is an important Allied asset in the cold war. Riots in East Germany and troubles in the satellites have widened the crack in Moscow's monolithic edifice of international communism.

In Europe, expanding and aggressive Russian communism abuts upon industrial communities whose standards of living are higher than those in Russia.

In Asia, Russia borders ancient and depressed lands with agrarian economies, whose standards of living are lower than those in the Communist motherland.

Eastern Siberian bases in Chukchi Peninsula and Kamchatka are closer to the continental United States than any other area under Russian control. These bases also threaten Alaska and the Aleutians and flank the great circle shipping and supply routes through the Pacific. Communists in Indo-China, China, Korea and Siberia hold most of the eastern coast of Asia, and Russian bases in Sakhalin and Kuriles are only a few hours distant by ship; a few minutes by plane from Hokkaido, northernmost Japanese island. Potentially, these continental and island positions "outflank" Japan and pose a threat of neutralization or conquest to the rich islands and archipelagoes fringing the coast. Conquest of South Korea would mean that Japan would be "outflanked" to the south as well as the north.

But Asia is a vast continent with few communications and seamed by deserts, towering mountain ranges, jungles and swamps. To a ground army the way of a conqueror would be hard. The Pacific is a far larger ocean than the Atlantic; Europe is closer to us than most of Asia.

Western Europe is a small homogeneous area, with few good defensive features, closely knit by modern communications, easily overrun by land armies. And today the Russian armies in the Eastern zone stand only seventy-five miles from the North Sea.

The basic politico-military strategy of, first, Britain, and then the United States, has been to prevent the domination of all of Europe and its sea gateways—the English Channel, the Skagerrak and the Strait of Gibraltar—by a single power. In the age of snorkel long-range submarines, guided missiles, long-range bombers and atomic arms this concept is even more important than in the past. Any viable defense of the United States—unless we want to fight a war in our skies or on our doorstep—must be based upon positions overseas.

Such bases, moreover, are essential to any successful offensive against Russia. Of all available overseas bases those in the British Isles, Iceland, Europe, North Africa and the Middle East are most important, since they are closest to vital Russian targets, and since they dominate the approaches to Germany—key to Europe. And the Mediterranean to the south and Arctic to the north offer sea flanking approaches to the Russian heartland which would permit us to capitalize upon our great superiority in naval power. There are no similar Pacific sea roads to the heart of Russia.

Morally and culturally Asia and Europe are as different as night from day. Yet it would be difficult to say that one is more resistant to communism than the other. Communism has traditionally developed its cancer among industrial workers. Europe is heavily industrialized; Asia is a land of peasants. Yet the largest Communist country (outside of Russia) is China. In one respect Asia is more vulnerable than Europe; the millions are ruled by a very small group of politicians and intellectuals, a group far easier to penetrate and control by communism, especially since most Asian politicians fear the "colonialism" of the West.

Asia (including its fringing islands) is more than five times as large as Europe; its estimated population is three times that of Europe. But in education, technological skills, organizational ability, political homogeneity and the utilization of machine power instead of manpower, Asia's peoples are decades and centuries behind Europe. Only one Pacific Asiatic power, Japan, so far has demonstrated the energy, discipline, organizational ability and technological skill to become a modern industrial state.

China may be emerging from her "long sleep," and if she is, Japan's remarkable progress in half a century from feudalism to industrialism may serve as a yardstick of China's future progress. But Asia's problems are major—religious taboos, tremendous birth rate, over-population, insufficient food, periodic famines, pestilence, ignorance, grossly inadequate communications; thousands of difficult languages and dialects; corrupt and inefficient governments; undeveloped economies mainly dependent upon a one-crop agriculture; weak leadership; factional, civil and national strife.

There is one common denominator, itself an enemy of communism—nationalism, expressed in part as a dislike for Western colonialism, which the so-called intellectuals and politicians of most Asiatic nations share. But this does not appear to be sufficient leaven to arouse quickly the whole vast mass of Asia; decades and perhaps centuries will be needed before the human resources of this great continent are really comparable to those of the West. In one sense—the sheer swarming hordes of manpower for use in mass armies or as cheap labor—Asia's tremendous population is an asset. But in another—its backwardness and low standards of living which focus most of Asia's energies on the struggle for existence—it is a liability.

The military asset of Asia's teeming manpower is not matched by military and technological development. Only Japan is capable of developing her own air and sea power; modern land weapons and the fighting ships and fighting planes of Asia are supplied by Russia or Western nations, and Asia has not really mastered their use.

The estimated steel production of all Asia (including Japan) in 1953 is 13,000,000 tons; that of free Europe (including Britain) is 72,000,000 tons. The power consumption of Europe is almost five times that of Asia, which contains nothing, for example, comparable to the Ruhr.

But when one compares the raw material wealth of Asia with that of Europe, the balance sheet is different. Asia produces vital supplies of petroleum, has a virtual monopoly on the production of natural rubber, and is the major producer of rice and tin, as well as large amounts of manganese. Exact estimates of Asia's mineral wealth are not available, as modern geological surveys have never investigated vast areas of the East. Yet it is fair to assume that there are vast untapped potentialities in the East which Europe apparently does not possess.

III. The Conclusions

Which then—Europe's machine power or Asia's manpower; Europe's industry or Asia's resources—is more important to the United States?

No categorical answer is possible; an equation of continent against continent cannot produce, in view of the human factors and the intangibles, an answer of mathematical precision. But it is clear that the conquest of Europe by communism would result in a far more immediate threat to the United States, and would have far more immediate worldwide repercussions than the conquest of Asia.

Europe is a rich prize of the present—a developed economy; Asia may make the history of tomorrow, but her strength is still potential and requires time for development. In a military sense Asia, with her millions, has a great defensive capability; Europe, with its vigorous, literate people and its machines, has an offensive capability. Europe today is a great market for American goods; Asia, a potential market. Western Europe and the United States have the same roots of culture, the same racial origins, the same basic Western Christian civilization; common customs and traditions unite us, while in Asia the ways are strange. The Atlantic-European area is, strategically, better suited to the exploitation of our superior sea and air power than is the Pacific-Asiatic theatre. Today, and for the foreseeable future, Europe is more important to the United States than Asia; tomorrow, if Asia realizes her potentialities, this judgment may be reversed.

There is, fortunately, no great conflict implicit in this judgment, as there was during World War II. For today Asia is the continent of the hot wars, and Asia should clearly have priority (as Korea and Indo-China have had) in the munitions needed to fight those wars, while Europe should have a high proportion of our economic and industrial aid which can make Europe (unlike Asia) militarily self-supporting.

But such judgments have little value except as a very general guide to American grand strategy. It is impossible to consider Europe apart from Asia, or vice versa. French rearmament is influenced greatly by the Indo-China war; Korean action has produced European reactions. Strategic localisms and sectionalisms are not possible in the atomic age. For the development of modern weapons and lines of communication means that the world today is truly round; the circle is joined. The map of the earth is foreshortened; both Atlantic and Pacific have shrunk in strategic terms to the dimensions of the English Channel, and even the polar icecap is no bar to aerial attack upon one continent by another—upon one hemisphere by another. As the power, the range and the speed of new weapons develop, the inexorable demands of global strategy will render more and more meaningless the insular and the isolationist point of view.

We must hold both Asia *and* Europe, and the keys today—the absolutely indispensable foci of our military, political and economic strategy—are Germany and Japan. Communism can win the world in Europe today, or in Asia tomorrow; there is no narrow simplified formula for victory in cold or hot wars.

Suggested Reading

There is no fully satisfactory diplomatic history of the political origins and nature of the Korean War, but several studies have been published which may be used as starting points for future work.

Stephen Ambrose, *Rise to Globalism: American Foreign Policy, 1938–1970,* Baltimore, Penguin Books, 1971 (paperback).

Roy E. Appleman, *South to the Naktong, North to the Yalu,* Washington, U.S. Government Printing Office, 1960.

Carl Berger, *The Korea Knot,* Philadelphia, University of Pennsylvania Press, 1957.

Leland M. Goodrich, *Korea: A Study of U.S. Policy in the United Nations,* New York, Council on Foreign Relations, 1956.

Glenn D. Paige, *The Korean Decision,* New York, Free Press, 1968 (paperback).

David Rees, *Korea: The Limited War,* New York, St. Martin's, 1964 (Penguin paperback).

Matthew Ridgway, *The Korean War,* New York, Doubleday, 1967 (Popular Library paperback).

Marshall D. Shulman, *Stalin's Foreign Policy Reappraised,* Cambridge, Mass., Harvard University Press, 1963 (Atheneum paperback).

John W. Spanier, *The Truman-MacArthur Controversy and the Korean War,* New York, Norton, 1965 (paperback).

I. F. Stone, *The Hidden History of the Korean War,* New York, Monthly Review Press, 1952, 1969 (paperback)

Index

A Note on the Editor

Lloyd C. Gardner was born in Delaware, Ohio, studied at Ohio Wesleyan University and the University of Wisconsin, and was a Woodrow Wilson Fellow. He is the author of the highly praised *Architects of Illusion: Men and Ideas in American Foreign Policy, 1941–1949,* and of *Economic Aspects of New Deal Diplomacy,* and editor of *A Different Frontier.* Mr. Gardner is now Professor of History at Rutgers University.